Scripture's Heroes and Villains

Scripture's Heroes and Villains

29 VOICES IN THEIR OWN DEFENSE

■ ■ ■

John J. Brugaletta

To the translators of the
World English Bible
for their generosity

I am also endebted to the following for their comments:

Claudia M. Brugaletta
John T. Brugaletta
Dr. Edward Curtis
Dr. Charles Dominick
William Elmore Gann
Bernard Giarratano
Dr. Patricia Hamilton
Dr. Stewart Long
Bonnie Oliver
Pastor Donald Schatz
Dr. Howard Seller
The Reverend Canon Mark Shier
Wm Erik Voss
Dr. Bruce H. Weber

Contents

General Introduction

■ ■ ■

A FAMOUS AMERICAN PREACHER OF our time once spent an entire sermon pointing out that motivation is of paramount importance in one's words and actions. And of course once we've thought about it, we can agree that, even though our actions and words *can* sometimes be harmful instead of helpful, if our motivation was to help, it would be difficult to blame us.

If an inexperienced cook is motivated by love and enthusiasm to bake a birthday cake for an ailing man, and she substitutes baking soda for baking powder without realizing the difference, is she guilty when the cake does not rise as it should? Of course not. On the other hand, if a man decides to murder another man, but the gun accidentally misfires, is he guilty in the eyes of God? Yes he is; it was not a part of his deadly decision for the gun to misfire (see Matthew 5:28). The only reason earthly law might hesitate to convict him of murder is that we human beings find it difficult to prove intent beyond a doubt.

But what we find throughout much of the Bible is silence on people's motivation, about the intention of someone whose actions are described. We know from circumstances that Abraham, after being promised a son, experiences something like anxiety when his son's birth is delayed. But the Bible does not explicitly say he was worried or anxious or confused (Genesis 15-17). We must deduce this from Abraham's circumstances and actions by asking ourselves what normal people would feel like in the case of such a clear promise, from an unimpeachable Source, with no results in sight.

Likewise we can assume that, in telling her two daughters-in-law to stay behind in Moab, their native country, Naomi is motivated either by her concern for their freedom from her unfruitful matriarchal influence, or that she is testing the young women's loyalty to her. But neither of these can be proven beyond a doubt from the book of Ruth.

It is this silence about motivation that gave rise to the following fictional (but plausible) monologues. In each case, I have striven to keep both justice and mercy in mind while searching for the person's reasons for saying and doing things; nevertheless, Bible commentator can never guarantee absolute accuracy in their interpretations. It may be that I have been too lenient or too harsh with some of these people, but that was my motivation for providing the relevant Scriptural passages in each case—so that the reader may more conveniently make up his or her mind about the accuracy of each monologue. I would be pleased to find that this has happened, because then this book will serve as great a purpose as if all of the monologues were found to be valid. For it is better to have read a biblical passage with the open eyes of curiosity than to read it with the half-closed eyes of a bored self-confidence.

Please keep in mind that the primary aim of this book is to provoke close study of the Bible, not a memorizing of canned answers. Too often, I believe, we read these biblical passages and, without realizing it, see the people in them as standing for something, rather than as human beings as real, as gifted, and as flawed as we ourselves are. If all we think of when we hear of Abraham is either his faith or his lack of it, we are neither doing him justice, nor deriving all of the spiritual benefits we can gain from reading the Bible. We are reducing these people to cardboard placards.

The theologian N.T.Wright has noted that "techniques of prayer and meditation have been known in all religions, not least in Judaism and Christianity themselves.... Many Christians today use the Ignatian method, taking a scriptural story and trying to 'get inside' it, living imaginatively within one of the parts in the drama and seeing what happens, hearing what God...says to you in the story" (*Acts for Everyone: Part One,* page 138). This is another way of looking at what this book is designed to do for the reader. In order to see what God says to you in the biblical passages at the beginning of each section of this book, be sure to finish each chapter by reading there, even if you have read it before. Try to hear the tones of voice of the monologue's speaker, whether sincere or snide, deceptive or candid. (Only the very young, in my experience, will find this difficult, for they tend to trust everyone.) This should give you a sense of reality in the Bible passages quoted.

J.J.B.

CHAPTER 1

Abraham

■ ■ ■

INTRODUCTION

In Romans 4:11, Paul speaks of the "righteousness that [Abraham] had by faith"; and in Galatians 3:7, he calls those who believe "children of Abraham." The author of Hebrews says in 11:8, "By faith Abraham, when called to go to a place he would later receive as his inheritance, obeyed and went...." And in 11:11, "By faith Abraham, even though he was past age—and Sarah herself was barren—was enabled to become a father...."

But there are people in our time who would say that Abraham, in having a son through Hagar, is to be considered less than faithful (Genesis 16:3-12). How can a believing reader of the Bible's account of Abraham's life reconcile these two positions? Is it simply a matter of choosing one part of the Bible or the other, or can one find a position on this patriarch that accounts for both?

See if you think the monologue that follows renders understandable this final position on the question.

ABRAHAM

MONOLOGUE

When I was told to circumcise them all, I carried out the order that same day. It is ingrained within me, this impatience to complete a task once it is set.

My father was near seventy when he implanted me within my mother's womb. And so when I was seventy-and-five and married several years, and still my wife received the seed and never bore a crop, my sheep, my oxen, camels, silver all were parching on my tongue: I had no son. All my possessions would descend upon a slave from Syria, one Eliezer who, conceived apart from me, was none of mine.

Then came the King of Elam to attack. When I and mine dispersed his army and retrieved my kin, Melchizedek brought out refreshing wine and bread, and blessed my head, and spoke of Adonai as my guard and strength. It was soon afterward that the One appeared and told me I would have a son and heir. And this I took as though accomplished, yet still in her locked womb untouched by proper key.

The months went by, and then the years. In time our storehouse of hope diminished as in a sequence of drought years. Mornings I'd venture out before the sun made visible this desert of my life. I'd pray to Elohim that He'd remember me in my affliction, bring rain upon my desolation, light to my uncomprehending mind.

When Sarai judged that I'd been balked enough, she put away her pride and offered me her slave, Egyptian Hagar as a wife. This was not every word Omnipotence had said should be, but I'd had little history with such immensity of promises. Could Sarai's name have been inserted as a test of my belief? So I went in to Hagar, and she conceived, and from enthusiasm that I do my best there sprang a wilderness of "donkeys" in the world.

It was not till my years were ninety-nine that we were told our son would, in the spring to come, be born to us—and we both dry, with old age drinking at our feeble veins. And in the spring he came like laughter's sound, like merriment when everyone has had his fill of bread, and wine is passed around, and thanks are given to the One on high for what He gives.

And only then did my blurred vision clear. I saw that passing on my sheep and cows were not my purpose, but it was this child, this evening birth of joy, this bursting pod of seeds to multiply my blessings wide and spangle earth the way night's sky is lit. And for that end no doubt I must await a longer, slower expectation's growth, until Melchizedek again shall bless the victory of Elohim in my seed.

ABRAHAM

GENESIS 16:

1 Now Sarai, Abram's wife, bore him no children. She had a servant, an Egyptian, whose name was Hagar. 2 Sarai said to Abram, "See now, God has restrained me from bearing. Please go in to my servant. It may be that I will obtain children by her." Abram listened to the voice of Sarai. 3 Sarai, Abram's wife, took Hagar the Egyptian, her servant, after Abram had lived ten years in the land of Canaan, and gave her to Abram her husband to be his wife. 4 He went in to Hagar, and she conceived.

12 He will be like a wild donkey among men. His hand will be against every man, and every man's hand against him. He will live opposed to all of his brothers."

GENESIS 17:

3 Abram fell on his face. God talked with him, saying, 4 "As for me, behold, my covenant is with you. You will be the father of a multitude of nations.

17 Then Abraham fell on his face, and laughed, and said in his heart, "Will a child be born to him who is one hundred years old? Will Sarah, who is ninety years old, give birth?" 18 Abraham said to God, "Oh that Ishmael might live before you!"

19 God said, "No, but Sarah, your wife, will bear you a son. You shall call his name Isaac. I will establish my covenant with him for an everlasting covenant for his offspring after him. 20 As for Ishmael, I have heard you. Behold, I have blessed him, and will make him fruitful, and will multiply him exceedingly. He will become the father of twelve

princes, and I will make him a great nation. 21 But I will establish my covenant with Isaac, whom Sarah will bear to you at this set time next year."

GENESIS 21:

1 God visited Sarah as he had said, and God did to Sarah as he had spoken. 2 Sarah conceived, and bore Abraham a son in his old age, at the set time of which God had spoken to him. 3 Abraham called his son who was born to him, whom Sarah bore to him, Isaac. * 4 Abraham circumcised his son, Isaac, when he was eight days old, as God had commanded him. 5 Abraham was one hundred years old when his son, Isaac, was born to him.

CHAPTER 2

Adam

■ ■ ■

INTRODUCTION

The *Anchor Bible* says, "In [Genesis 2 and 3], everything is transposed into human terms....[What is] evoked is the childhood of mankind itself" (vol. 1, page 25). When seen from this perspective, we may be justified in asking why God would place such a source of forbidden fruit "in the middle of the garden," and evidently told the couple its location (Genesis 3:3). Surely ordinary children in biblical times were as inquisitive about forbidden things as children are today.

Was this situation the first test of mankind's obedience? Clearly, yes. Was it likely to succeed in keeping our first parents in Eden forever? No, not likely, given the forbidden fruit's easy accessibility, even if the serpentine tempter had never been involved.

So once again, why does God place the temptation within easy reach of the pair? Was it because God was testing our free will? C.S. Lewis writes, "If a thing is free to be good, it is also free to be bad. And free will is what has made evil possible." And then Lewis asks, "Why, then, did God give [us humans] free will? Because free will, though it makes evil possible, is also the only thing that makes possible any love or goodness or joy worth having" (*Mere Christianity*, page 53).

If these motivations are behind the scenes of Genesis 2 and 3, then we are brought to yet another example of God's loving-kindness, wanting his human children to be fully and completely alive, yet grieving (as any loving parent would) over the consequent ills and heartaches that will be their lot.

And by the way, notice how this view changes God's so-called "punishments" (bearing children in pain and working up a sweat to earn food) into mere descriptions of the circumstances surrounding the choice they have made.

ADAM

Monologue

How little we both knew before the Turn—the loosing of us on adulthood, its wails of anguish or the silent and insistent ache that we had been discarded. the Lord's single law: Avoid that one banned tree and what it bore. Unseeing that we were, we knew the present moment and no more. The suggestion came, and we both bit that most delicious fruit, but in our different ways; she to know, and I for love of her.

And so with guilt to either motivate our lives or mumble us into despair, we left like children come of age sent out to seek our fortune in a wilderness. Now it was not one lone fruit forbidden in a nursery of liberalities, but rather isolated freedoms in a system dressed with illegalities. We may not take a cup that's not our own, while others may, with brash impunity, confiscate what should be ours alone: our garden's yield, our home, our only robe. We should—ah no, we must—tell truth itself, no matter that it could abort our lives, but lightning never strikes the willful teller of untruths.

These and so many more. Old age's bitter harvest of debilities, ingratitude of offspring, tactless parents, swindling merchants, thieving customers, burglars, rapists, smugglers, pimps, judges who are self-concerned, the courtly talker with a base agenda.

The question of entrapment locked our every thought. Then Eve first posed the key. In speaking of that "tantalizing and delicious fruit within our crib," she held her peace at "crib" and asked of me, What had we been today if we had not transgressed? A race of toddlers in the tropics, no wiser than pubescent striplings are; loyal cattle, and with their vacant mind, unseparated yet from half-blind following of rules, a pair of puppets at the ends of strings.

ADAM

GENESIS 2:

7 God formed man from the dust of the ground, and breathed into his nostrils the breath of life; and man became a living soul. 8 God planted a garden eastward, in Eden, and there he put the man whom he had formed. 9 Out of the ground God made every tree to grow that is pleasant to the sight, and good for food, including the tree of life in the middle of the garden and the tree of the knowledge of good and evil. 10 A river went out of Eden to water the garden; and from there it was parted, and became the source of four rivers. 11 The name of the first is Pishon: it flows through the whole land of Havilah, where there is gold; 12 and the gold of that land is good. Bdellium and onyx stone are also there. 13 The name of the second river is Gihon. It is the same river that flows through the whole land of Cush. 14 The name of the third river is Hiddekel. This is the one which flows in front of Assyria. The fourth river is the Euphrates. 15 God took the man, and put him into the garden of Eden to cultivate and keep it. 16 God commanded the man, saying, "You may freely eat of every tree of the garden; 17 but you shall not eat of the tree of the knowledge of good and evil; for in the day that you eat of it, you will surely die."

18 God said, "It is not good for the man to be alone. I will make him a helper comparable to him." 19 Out of the ground God formed every animal of the field, and every bird of the sky, and brought them to the man to see what he would call them. Whatever the man called every living creature became its name. 20 The man gave names to all livestock, and to the birds of the sky, and to every animal of the field; but for man there was not found a helper comparable to him. 21 God caused the man to fall into a deep sleep. As the man slept, he took one

of his ribs, and closed up the flesh in its place. 22 God made a woman from the rib which he had taken from the man, and brought her to the man. 23 The man said, "This is now bone of my bones, and flesh of my flesh. She will be called 'woman,' because she was taken out of Man." 24 Therefore a man will leave his father and his mother, and will join with his wife, and they will be one flesh.

CHAPTER 3

Bathsheba

■ ■ ■

INTRODUCTION

In ancient monarchies, a dying king's word would often influence heavily the choice of his successor. But political maneuvering worked its way into the choice as well. The dying king's advisors and others in the palace community, along with a politically minded wife, could exert their will on the transition of power.

This might be applied to the two people who bring Solomon to the throne of Israel, the prophet Nathan and Solomon's mother Bathsheba. In 2 Samuel 12, Nathan is sent by God to David in order to convince the King of his guilt in the killing of Uriah. In 1 Kings 1:10-21, however, there is no indication that Nathan is acting under God's command in using his position to put Solomon on the throne after David dies. In fact, in verse 10, it is reasonably clear that Nathan has his own political agenda.

This is not to say that Nathan is wicked in this instance, only that he is acting on his own. And in verses 11-21 we see that Bathsheba is easily persuaded to act on behalf of Solomon, her oldest living son by David.

If all this is accurate, we might apply it to her younger days by asking a few questions about her first encounter with David: Did she know that King David had stayed at home that spring, when kings normally went with their armies to war? (2 Samuel 1:1) Did she know that she was attractive? (1:2b) Did she realize that she could be seen from the roof of

David's palace while bathing in her garden? Could the wife of a humble soldier resist a king's sexual advances? Might the wife of a soldier wish for an opportunity to become a wife of a king? Where does this lead you in your estimation of Bathsheba's motives?

Finally, if a reader's first reaction to these speculations about Bathsheba's motives should be disturbing, I have two requests: (1) Remember that these are speculations with which you should feel free to disagree, and (2) Try to compare her with England's Queen Elizabeth I, a woman extremely capable of political strategems and deceptive techniques for her survival as queen. Had Shakespeare's Hotspur been her contemporary, he might have called her a "vile politician," but we today see her as a heroine of history.

BATHSHEBA

MONOLOGUE

It was warm spring. Uriah was away in Rabbah killing Ammonites, and I had longed all winter for the water's tongue to lick me with its trickle down my back. My servants babbled of the King at home, his near demise in battle, Abishai to rescue him. They spoke of cautions afterward to send the lesser men to war and keep the lamp of Israel alight at home. I thought it interesting. It was my time of cleansing, and I bade my girls transport my bath into the garden as the sun reclined in tender luminance to bed.

A royal summons came. I must attend. In my demurest gown, and faint of scent, they led me and my maids to kingly heights where soon the girls were lured to wine and cates, and I to conversation with the King. His speech was tender, then was strong by turns. How can a subject woman countermand the urging admiration of her king?

These privacies, however, soon would bear a public manifest. I held within my proper reticence a regal charge. I called my Anna, taught her to say my words exact, and sent her Davidward. She was of age declined enough to be a flesh he would ignore yet listen to. She was to speak Uriah's absence and the consequent endangerment of me, with merest hint of scandal otherwise.

Soon Uriah was back from war's embrace and close in audience. When drained of facts, their place filled up with wine, he staggered home and stood before the gate in drunken indecision on the soldier's code: one way to continence in wartime, the other to the King's command to wash his "feet" in wifely succulence. He might have entered in, but Anna soon reminded him his men would scorn the lapse.

And so there was no remedy for all but that the Hittite die in battle's arms. And that was how my innocence had come to rise above my modest origins and bear at last a wiser king, her son. Of how this wisdom should perpetuate, I claim no recognition, only that the choicest line will bear the choicest son.

2 SAMUEL 11:

1 At the return of the year, at the time when kings go out, David sent Joab, and his servants with him, and all Israel; and they destroyed the children of Ammon, and besieged Rabbah. But David stayed at Jerusalem. 2 At evening, David arose from his bed and walked on the roof of the king's house. From the roof, he saw a woman bathing, and the woman was very beautiful to look at. 3 David sent and inquired after the woman. One said, "Isn't this Bathsheba, the daughter of Eliam, Uriah the Hittite's wife?"

4 David sent messengers, and took her; and she came in to him, and he lay with her (for she was purified from her uncleanness); and she returned to her house. 5 The woman conceived; and she sent and told David, and said, "I am with child."

6 David sent to Joab, "Send me Uriah the Hittite." Joab sent Uriah to David. 7 When Uriah had come to him, David asked him how Joab did, and how the people fared, and how the war prospered. 8 David said to Uriah, "Go down to your house and wash your feet." Uriah departed

out of the king's house, and a gift from the king was sent after him. 9 But Uriah slept at the door of the king's house with all the servants of his lord, and didn't go down to his house.

2 SAMUEL 11:

26 When Uriah's wife heard that Uriah her husband was dead, she mourned for her husband. 27 When the mourning was past, David sent and took her home to his house, and she became his wife, and bore him a son. But the thing that David had done displeased God.

1 KINGS 1:

11 Then Nathan spoke to Bathsheba the mother of Solomon, saying, "Haven't you heard that Adonijah the son of Haggith reigns, and David our lord doesn't know it? 12 Now therefore come, please let me give you counsel, that you may save your own life, and your son Solomon's life. 13 Go in to king David, and tell him, 'Didn't you, my lord, king, swear to your servant, saying, "Assuredly Solomon your son shall reign after me, and he shall sit on my throne?" Why then does Adonijah reign?' 14 Behold, while you are still talking there with the king, I will also come in after you and confirm your words."

15 Bathsheba went in to the king in his room. The king was very old; and Abishag the Shunammite was serving the king. 16 Bathsheba bowed, and showed respect to the king. The king said, "What would you like?"

17 She said to him, "My lord, you swore by God your God to your servant, 'Assuredly Solomon your son shall reign after me, and he shall sit on my throne.' 18 Now, behold, Adonijah reigns; and you, my lord the king, don't know it. 19 He has slain cattle and fatlings and sheep in abundance, and has called all the sons of the king, Abiathar the priest, and Joab the captain of the army; but he hasn't called Solomon your servant. 20 You, my lord the king, the eyes of all Israel are on you, that you should tell them who will sit on the throne of my lord the king after

him. 21 Otherwise it will happen, when my lord the king sleeps with his fathers, that I and my son Solomon will be considered criminals."

22 Behold, while she was still talking with the king, Nathan the prophet came in. 23 They told the king, saying, "Behold, Nathan the prophet!"

When he had come in before the king, he bowed himself before the king with his face to the ground. 24 Nathan said, "My lord, king, have you said, 'Adonijah shall reign after me, and he shall sit on my throne?' 25 For he has gone down today, and has slain cattle, fatlings, and sheep in abundance, and has called all the king's sons, the captains of the army, and Abiathar the priest. Behold, they are eating and drinking before him, and saying, 'Long live king Adonijah!' 26 But he hasn't called me, even me your servant, Zadok the priest, Benaiah the son of Jehoiada, and your servant Solomon. 27 Was this thing done by my lord the king, and you haven't shown to your servants who should sit on the throne of my lord the king after him?"

28 Then king David answered, "Call Bathsheba in to me." She came into the king's presence and stood before the king. 29 The king swore, and said, "As God lives, who has redeemed my soul out of all adversity, 30 most certainly as I swore to you by God, the God of Israel, saying, 'Assuredly Solomon your son shall reign after me, and he shall sit on my throne in my place;' I will most certainly do this today."

31 Then Bathsheba bowed with her face to the earth, and showed respect to the king, and said, "Let my lord king David live forever!"

CHAPTER 4

Cain

■ ■ ■

INTRODUCTION

Just as there is no visible cause for Job's miseries, or at least no cause visible to him, there seems at first glance to be no visible cause for God's refusal of Cain's offering. We are therefore cautioned by some Bible commentaries to abandon such a search and to ask instead, "How does one respond when God says no?"

But before we try to follow this advice, let's recall Jesus' challenge to the rich young ruler. The man asks what he "must do to inherit eternal life?" (Mark 10:17). Jesus' answer displays the fact that He knew the man's problem before he had even asked the question: "One thing you lack.... Go, sell everything you have and give to the poor" (10:21). The rich man's face falls, and he walks away.

Here too, as early as the fourth chapter of Genesis, God knows Cain's heart is filled with anger, and his face too is "downcast" (4:6). But God allows Cain the choice of either acting on his anger or mastering it. He acts on it, murdering his innocent brother Abel, and God sentences him to exile, the greatest punishment for an ancient Jew.

It seems there may be a cause after all for God's refusal of Cain's offering. Could it be to give him a test on his known weakness so as to bring it out into the open where it may be dealt with in one way or another?

But notice please that even after Cain has failed the test, God's love protects him with a mark (4:15).

CAIN

MONOLOGUE

Sap, dupe, simpleton of youth, this sheep-man, this gullible and guileless dolt. With greasy hands, he piled their haunches on the logs. Up went his smoke like a smile from Elohim. On my neat handful of the choicest grain He frowned. My rejected smoke aggrieved my eyes. They burned and ran. That I, a peaceful man, should have my offering pushed in my face while this thin boy was embraced—this ignited me.

A sounding voice. It must have been the old who chant the same: "No anger. Keep your cheer and you will be uplifted. Failing in that, your wolfish snarls await you at your door. They seek to devour you. Be lord of them." But they knew no such desire as burned my throat. If kind Ubiquity was the source of this, He was too sweet for such a man care-laden as I am.

I spoke to Abel fair, proposed a walk. I saw his eye. It said he pitied me. But it was he whose *life* afflicted me. With him cut off, I'd be sole supplicant. In no one's sight, I lay in two his throat. The head went rolling, writing blood in earth. The letters said, "Where is your brother now?" He nothing was the boy who'd skipped and laughed. No, no, consider me no guardian. My brother, though a sheep, was not within my charge.

But now the soil spat my seeds back at me. There was a taint on it. Earth's womb was closed. I left. There was more world for me to walk. Hopeless men, their hands on knives, looked on my face and turned away. I found a wife. I founded a city. I never have found peace.

CAIN

GENESIS 4:

1 The man knew Eve his wife. She conceived, and gave birth to Cain, and said, "I have gotten a man with God's help." 2 Again she gave birth, to Cain's brother Abel. Abel was a keeper of sheep, but Cain was a tiller

of the ground. 3 As time passed, Cain brought an offering to God from the fruit of the ground. 4 Abel also brought some of the firstborn of his flock and of its fat. God respected Abel and his offering, 5 but he didn't respect Cain and his offering. Cain was very angry, and the expression on his face fell. 6 God said to Cain, "Why are you angry? Why has the expression of your face fallen? 7 If you do well, won't it be lifted up? If you don't do well, sin crouches at the door. Its desire is for you, but you are to rule over it." 8 Cain said to Abel, his brother, "Let's go into the field." While they were in the field, Cain rose up against Abel, his brother, and killed him.

9 God said to Cain, "Where is Abel, your brother?"

He said, "I don't know. Am I my brother's keeper?"

10 God said, "What have you done? The voice of your brother's blood cries to me from the ground. 11 Now you are cursed because of the ground, which has opened its mouth to receive your brother's blood from your hand. 12 From now on, when you till the ground, it won't yield its strength to you. You will be a fugitive and a wanderer in the earth."

13 Cain said to God, "My punishment is greater than I can bear. 14 Behold, you have driven me out today from the surface of the ground. I will be hidden from your face, and I will be a fugitive and a wanderer in the earth. Whoever finds me will kill me."

15 God said to him, "Therefore whoever slays Cain, vengeance will be taken on him sevenfold." God appointed a sign for Cain, so that anyone finding him would not strike him.

16 Cain left God's presence, and lived in the land of Nod, east of Eden.

CHAPTER 5

David

■ ■ ■

INTRODUCTION

It seems that no man in the Old Testament, not Abraham, not Moses, and not David, lived a life completely under the approval of God. Though all were admirable in many respects, sinless they were not. (Only Jesus could eventually attain to a faultless life.) Abraham had bred with Hagar; Moses had failed to honor God in the Desert of Zin; and now David errs in his adulterous relationship with Bathsheba and his murder of Uriah.

And yet God fitted each of these imperfect men into his plan for the new Kingdom to be inaugurated by Jesus: Abraham was the first person to take up and maintain the worship of the one true God instead of the idols of Ur; Moses led the Israelites out of Egyptian slavery and within sight of the promised land; and David, having been chosen to save Saul's army from the Philistine champion, went on to father a line of sons that led to Jesus, the only Son of God.

DAVID

MONOLOGUE

My crushing of Goliath was no major feat of mine. I merely kept my eye fixed on his head and then released the stone just where I looked. There's a shepherd keeping every flock of sheep who can do as well, if only he should be presented with the circumstances I was given from on high.

My stone pulled down the too-tall man unto a stupor, and once he lay supine, I released his head. Nothing difficult. The sovereign thing was to position someone like me and my sling onto the battlefield at just the moment all things had been set—the challenge for two champions to meet, my arriving from the flock, my slender youth to cause the giant's resulting over-confidence. All that, the Lord did, not I.

Of course I took much courage from that victory, and courage based on the Lord's favor is a weapon that will seldom fail. So when it does appear to fail...well, I suppose it means we are not, at that moment, woven into the will of the Lord's plan.

And that brings to mind the taking of Bathsheba to my bed. I'd taken my advisors' counsel to abstain from battle that disastrous spring, and I was bored. My food was tasteless and my lyre spoke nothing sweet. At its start, I told myself her naked visibility in bathing was a sign to me. How could I refuse the Lord's discerning gift, discerning, that is to say, of my ennui and rising pressure of my lust.

But later, when wise Nathan showed me how I'd erred, I saw it was alone my appetite for woman's beauty that commanded my commands. Yet by that time she had inhabited the breath of me; and from that time, my word with family caused smiles behind their hands. Who could respect a father when a mother sat the throne?

She led my "feet" thereafter, as the ox-herd leads a bull by that brass ring within its nose. It was my tender feet the courtiers had in mind when they brought youthful Abishag to warm my cooling flesh. For even that old source of warmth had passed away, and I was left..., forgiven, yes, but thought untrustworthy by the Ruler of all things. Abandoned, dried and weakened, my only hope was that the Lord remember me and not discard what good I'd done.

DAVID

1 SAMUEL 13:

1 Saul was thirty years old when he became king, and he reigned over Israel forty-two years. 2 Saul chose for himself three thousand men of

Israel, of which two thousand were with Saul in Michmash and in the Mount of Bethel, and one thousand were with Jonathan in Gibeah of Benjamin. He sent the rest of the people to their own tents. 3 Jonathan struck the garrison of the Philistines that was in Geba, and the Philistines heard of it. Saul blew the trumpet throughout all the land, saying, "Let the Hebrews hear!" 4 All Israel heard that Saul had struck the garrison of the Philistines, and also that Israel was considered an abomination to the Philistines. The people were gathered together after Saul to Gilgal. 5 The Philistines assembled themselves together to fight with Israel, thirty thousand chariots, and six thousand horsemen, and people as the sand which is on the seashore in multitude. They came up and encamped in Michmash, eastward of Beth Aven. 6 When the men of Israel saw that they were in trouble (for the people were distressed), then the people hid themselves in caves, in thickets, in rocks, in tombs, and in pits. 7 Now some of the Hebrews had gone over the Jordan to the land of Gad and Gilead; but as for Saul, he was yet in Gilgal, and all the people followed him trembling. 8 He stayed seven days, according to the time set by Samuel; but Samuel didn't come to Gilgal, and the people were scattering from him. 9 Saul said, "Bring the burnt offering to me here, and the peace offerings." He offered the burnt offering.

10 It came to pass that as soon as he had finished offering the burnt offering, behold, Samuel came; and Saul went out to meet him, that he might greet him. 11 Samuel said, "What have you done?"

Saul said, "Because I saw that the people were scattered from me, and that you didn't come within the days appointed, and that the Philistines assembled themselves together at Michmash; 12 therefore I said, 'Now the Philistines will come down on me to Gilgal, and I haven't entreated the favor of God.' I forced myself therefore, and offered the burnt offering."

13 Samuel said to Saul, "You have done foolishly. You have not kept the commandment of your God, which he commanded you; for now God would have established your kingdom on Israel forever. 14 But now your

kingdom will not continue. God has sought for himself a man after his own heart, and God has appointed him to be prince over his people, because you have not kept that which God commanded you."

15 Samuel arose, and went from Gilgal to Gibeah of Benjamin. Saul counted the people who were present with him, about six hundred men. 16 Saul, and Jonathan his son, and the people who were present with them, stayed in Geba of Benjamin; but the Philistines encamped in Michmash. 17 The raiders came out of the camp of the Philistines in three companies: one company turned to the way that leads to Ophrah, to the land of Shual; 18 another company turned the way to Beth Horon; and another company turned the way of the border that looks down on the valley of Zeboim toward the wilderness. 19 Now there was no blacksmith found throughout all the land of Israel; for the Philistines said, "Lest the Hebrews make themselves swords or spears"; 20 but all the Israelites went down to the Philistines, each man to sharpen his own plowshare, mattock, ax, and sickle. 21 The price was one payim each to sharpen mattocks, plowshares, pitchforks, axes, and goads. 22 So it came to pass in the day of battle, that neither sword nor spear was found in the hand of any of the people who were with Saul and Jonathan; but Saul and Jonathan his son had them.

CHAPTER 6

Herod Antipas

■ ■ ■

INTRODUCTION

This Herod was not Herod the Great, the king who interviewed the Magi at the time of the Nativity and tried to kill Jesus as an infant. The Herod we are considering here was one of his sons, a Tetrarch* who ruled while Jesus was an adult.

It's interesting to watch this second Herod as he tries to interview Jesus, who was sent to him as a prisoner by Pilate. There was not much love lost between the two leaders, but Pilate might have been trying to mend fences with Herod by asking Herod's opinion on the case. Of course Pilate may also have been anxious to avoid ordering Jesus' execution himself, so he might have been hoping Herod would make that decision for him. In either case, Herod would be fully aware of how unusual the gesture was, coming from Pilate.

But it is even more interesting that Herod feared that John the Baptist had come back to life, and that clearly troubled him. Here we find what may be the kernel of Herod's personality: *He has a troubled conscience.* This may be seen as a result of two incidents. First, his imprisonment of John for criticizing his marriage to his sister-in-law and niece, Herodias. And second, his having been forced to behead John, whom he feared, because of his drunken promise to Herodias's daughter.

*a governor of a fourth part of an ancient province

HEROD ANTIPAS

MONOLOGUE

My ears deployed have heard him call me "fox," so when the Procurator passed him on, I grasped this piece of chance to ascertain if he had meant I'm clever. If so, I'm sure I could find a use for his miracles as tools of my estate.

And so, He standing there before my chair of state, I told my slave that I would see a sign. (I find my dignity's preserved by keeping my subordinates between the rabble and myself.) I saw that He knew it was a command from me, but held his tongue and moved no hand's breadth to obey my will. I told my slave, "Insist." To no avail.

My court was gathered to observe his magic tricks and, seeing none, were bored and turned to scattered whisperings. I looked to see if there was something like a scar upon his neck where my slave's ax beheaded him, but there was none of that either. The gathering's continued whisperings produced a nice distraction, which I exploited to examine him on politics and plans. He answered nothing, which I took as sign he was abashed, or else retarded in his thought. This only was my entertaining sign, and entertained alone myself.

He'd been a gift from Pilate, so I owed one in return. His own returned unharmed, except my smile's erosion of his pride. One cannot be too careful on one's throne. The throng is put in awe by temples built, but probing words can pull them on one's head. And that brings back to me again my lack of certainty as to what use John's followers have put his severed head.

HEROD ANTIPAS

MATTHEW 14:

1 At that time, Herod the tetrarch heard the report concerning Jesus, 2 and said to his servants, "This is John the Baptizer. He is risen from the dead. That is why these powers work in him." 3 For Herod had

laid hold of John, and bound him, and put him in prison for the sake of Herodias, his brother Philip's wife. 4 For John said to him, "It is not lawful for you to have her." 5 When he would have put him to death, he feared the multitude, because they counted him as a prophet. 6 But when Herod's birthday came, the daughter of Herodias danced among them and pleased Herod. 7 Whereupon he promised with an oath to give her whatever she should ask. 8 She, being prompted by her mother, said, "Give me here on a platter the head of John the Baptizer."

9 The king was grieved, but for the sake of his oaths, and of those who sat at the table with him, he commanded it to be given, 10 and he sent and beheaded John in the prison. 11 His head was brought on a platter, and given to the young lady: and she brought it to her mother. 12 His disciples came, and took the body, and buried it; and they went and told Jesus.

MARK 6:

14 King Herod heard this, for his name had become known, and he said, "John the Baptizer has risen from the dead, and therefore these powers are at work in him." 15 But others said, "He is Elijah." Others said, "He is a prophet, or like one of the prophets." 16 But Herod, when he heard this, said, "This is John, whom I beheaded. He has risen from the dead." 17 For Herod himself had sent out and arrested John, and bound him in prison for the sake of Herodias, his brother Philip's wife, for he had married her. 18 For John said to Herod, "It is not lawful for you to have your brother's wife." 19 Herodias set herself against him, and desired to kill him, but she couldn't, 20 for Herod feared John, knowing that he was a righteous and holy man, and kept him safe. When he heard him, he did many things, and he heard him gladly.

21 Then a convenient day came, that Herod on his birthday made a supper for his nobles, the high officers, and the chief men of Galilee. 22 When the daughter of Herodias herself came in and danced, she

pleased Herod and those sitting with him. The king said to the young lady, "Ask me whatever you want, and I will give it to you." 23 He swore to her, "Whatever you shall ask of me, I will give you, up to half of my kingdom."

24 She went out, and said to her mother, "What shall I ask?"
She said, "The head of John the Baptizer."

25 She came in immediately with haste to the king, and asked, "I want you to give me right now the head of John the Baptizer on a platter."

26 The king was exceedingly sorry, but for the sake of his oaths, and of his dinner guests, he didn't wish to refuse her. 27 Immediately the king sent out a soldier of his guard, and commanded to bring John's head, and he went and beheaded him in the prison, 28 and brought his head on a platter, and gave it to the young lady; and the young lady gave it to her mother.

29 When his disciples heard this, they came and took up his corpse, and laid it in a tomb.

LUKE 3:

19 but Herod the tetrarch, being reproved by him for Herodias, his brother's wife, and for all the evil things which Herod had done, 20 added this also to them all, that he shut up John in prison.

LUKE 9:

7 Now Herod the tetrarch heard of all that was done by him; and he was very perplexed, because it was said by some that John had risen from the dead, 8 and by some that Elijah had appeared, and by others that one of the old prophets had risen again. 9 Herod said, "John I beheaded, but who is this about whom I hear such things?" He sought to see him.

LUKE 13:

31 On that same day, some Pharisees came, saying to him, "Get out of here, and go away, for Herod wants to kill you."

32 He said to them, "Go and tell that fox, 'Behold, I cast out demons and perform cures today and tomorrow, and the third day I complete my mission. 33 Nevertheless I must go on my way today and tomorrow and the next day, for it can't be that a prophet would perish outside of Jerusalem.'

LUKE 23:

6 But when Pilate heard Galilee mentioned, he asked if the man was a Galilean. 7 When he found out that he was in Herod's jurisdiction, he sent him to Herod, who was also in Jerusalem during those days.

8 Now when Herod saw Jesus, he was exceedingly glad, for he had wanted to see him for a long time, because he had heard many things about him. He hoped to see some miracle done by him. 9 He questioned him with many words, but he gave no answers. 10 The chief priests and the scribes stood, vehemently accusing him. 11 Herod with his soldiers humiliated him and mocked him. Dressing him in luxurious clothing, they sent him back to Pilate. 12 Herod and Pilate became friends with each other that very day, for before that they were enemies with each other.

13 Pilate called together the chief priests, the rulers, and the people, 14 and said to them, "You brought this man to me as one that perverts the people, and behold, having examined him before you, I found no basis for a charge against this man concerning those things of which you accuse him. 15 Neither has Herod, for I sent you to him, and see, nothing worthy of death has been done by him.

ACTS 12:

1 Now about that time, King Herod stretched out his hands to oppress some of the assembly. 2 He killed James, the brother of John, with the sword. 3 When he saw that it pleased the Jews, he proceeded to seize Peter also. This was during the days of unleavened bread. 4 When he had arrested him, he put him in prison, and delivered him to four squads of four soldiers each to guard him, intending to bring him out

to the people after the Passover. 5 Peter therefore was kept in the prison, but constant prayer was made by the assembly to God for him. 6 The same night when Herod was about to bring him out, Peter was sleeping between two soldiers, bound with two chains. Guards in front of the door kept the prison....

18 Now as soon as it was day, there was no small stir among the soldiers about what had become of Peter. 19 When Herod had sought for him, and didn't find him, he examined the guards, then commanded that they should be put to death. He went down from Judea to Caesarea, and stayed there. 20 Now Herod was very angry with the people of Tyre and Sidon. They came with one accord to him, and, having made Blastus, the king's personal aide, their friend, they asked for peace, because their country depended on the king's country for food. 21 On an appointed day, Herod dressed himself in royal clothing, sat on the throne, and gave a speech to them. 22 The people shouted, "The voice of a god, and not of a man!" 23 Immediately an angel of the Lord struck him, because he didn't give God the glory. Then he was eaten by worms and died.

CHAPTER 7

Isaac

■ ■ ■

INTRODUCTION

Someone once wrote about a boy who had heard his teacher tell the class about the kinds of snakes that are relatively "harmless." But when the boy tried to repeat for his family what his teacher had said, he pronounced "harmless" as "armless," and so revealing to his parents how he had misunderstood. He said he didn't know why she called them armless. Weren't *all* snakes armless—and legless too?

While children can be both honest and perceptive, their verbal mistakes can also be funny, as well as being able to savor a good practical joke. This is how the monologue presents the young Isaac (whose name means laughter) as he follows his father Abraham to sacrifice a "sheep" on a pyre.

For Abraham, in all his understandable grief, the sheep is Isaac, but clearly he has not told the boy this (perhaps to shorten what he expects to be Isaac's period of fright, or perhaps because he has not yet found out if he really can obey God's command to sacrifice Isaac). And so, as sometimes happens with children, Isaac mistakes his father's tying him up as the first time the dignified patriarch has joked with him—a type of interaction he may have experienced in wrestling playfully with servants his age.

By the way, Isaac's monologue is meant to be read as his telling of the incident shortly after it happened, that is, while he is still very young.

ISAAC

MONOLOGUE

My dad split so much wood that I said please I needed help to carry it. So Phicol and Ephron went along. We started early. Hamor stood quiet while I saddled him, then Dad got on and we got started for the heights.

The servants hung behind and talked in whispers, because my dad said "Silence" twice, but I could hear them. Ephron said, "Hey, how come we never brung no lamb?" And I began to joke about what Dad would sacrifice. "Me, maybe," I said, "or maybe some bird or lizard. Might be hard tying up a lizard with this rope." I couldn't keep from laughing, till my dad gave me a look. So I got too far behind for him to hear me.

It took three days. I saw a hill ahead. Dad told the servants to stay there with Hamor. I carried all the wood. It was hard, but Dad and I walked on. We didn't talk. Then I saw a lizard. That reminded me of Ephron's question about the lamb. I almost asked Dad if that was what we would sacrifice, but then I felt a giggle coming up, so I changed the words. "Dad," I said, "how come we brought no lamb?" He said, "God will provide the lamb, my son,"

And then Dad played the best joke of them all: he tied *me* up and played like I was it. He was joking with me. Did that mean I was a man? I went, "Baa, baa," and acted like a sheep. But then I looked at Dad, and he looked serious. I thought, "Boy, I bet fire hurts. Oh well, Dad knows what he's doing."

And that's when he saw the sheep he talked about, caught in some thorn bushes. He took away the ropes, and he and I took hold of it, a ram. I guess I wasn't grown enough to take the fire.

ISAAC

GENESIS 22:

1 After these things, God tested Abraham, and said to him, "Abraham!"
He said, "Here I am."

2 He said, "Now take your son, your only son, Isaac, whom you love, and go into the land of Moriah. Offer him there as a burnt offering on one of the mountains which I will tell you of."

3 Abraham rose early in the morning, and saddled his donkey; and took two of his young men with him, and Isaac his son. He split the wood for the burnt offering, and rose up, and went to the place of which God had told him. 4 On the third day Abraham lifted up his eyes, and saw the place far off. 5 Abraham said to his young men, "Stay here with the donkey. The boy and I will go yonder. We will worship, and come back to you." 6 Abraham took the wood of the burnt offering and laid it on Isaac his son. He took in his hand the fire and the knife. They both went together. 7 Isaac spoke to Abraham his father, and said, "My father?"

He said, "Here I am, my son."

He said, "Here is the fire and the wood, but where is the lamb for a burnt offering?"

8 Abraham said, "God will provide himself the lamb for a burnt offering, my son." So they both went together. 9 They came to the place which God had told him of. Abraham built the altar there, and laid the wood in order, bound Isaac his son, and laid him on the altar, on the wood. 10 Abraham stretched out his hand, and took the knife to kill his son.

11 God's angel called to him out of the sky, and said, "Abraham, Abraham!"

He said, "Here I am."

12 He said, "Don't lay your hand on the boy or do anything to him. For now I know that you fear God, since you have not withheld your son, your only son, from me."

13 Abraham lifted up his eyes, and looked, and saw that behind him was a ram caught in the thicket by his horns. Abraham went and took the ram, and offered him up for a burnt offering instead of his son. 14 Abraham called the name of that place "God Will Provide". As it is said to this day, "On God's mountain, it will be provided."

15 God's angel called to Abraham a second time out of the sky, 16 and said, " 'I have sworn by myself,' says God, 'because you have done this thing, and have not withheld your son, your only son, 17 that I will bless you greatly, and I will multiply your offspring greatly like the stars of the heavens, and like the sand which is on the seashore. Your offspring will possess the gate of his enemies. 18 All the nations of the earth will be blessed by your offspring, because you have obeyed my voice.' "

19 So Abraham returned to his young men, and they rose up and went together to Beersheba. Abraham lived at Beersheba.

CHAPTER 8

Jacob

■ ■ ■

INTRODUCTION

In dealing with Jacob's personality, we must begin with the contrast between him and his fraternal twin, Esau. The latter is a man of the hills and wild animals, a hunter and a plain, forthright man, not given to duplicity. Jacob is his brother's opposite in almost every way; he is a "man of the tents," living a life filled with cunning and deceit; a herdsman. As such, the two brothers may be meant to represent two successive phases in the development of the human race: the simpler and more primitive hunter as distinct from the somewhat more sophisticated and social herdsman.

Admittedly this picture of humanity's changing mode of survival is stereotyped and perhaps sentimental, but it seems to be the writer's opinion in view of the fact that the word Esau uses in Genesis 25:30, where he says to Jacob, "Give me a swallow of that red stuff, for I am starving." Because in addition to meaning "swallow," the Hebrew word used can also mean "gulp down" (E.A. Speiser, *The Anchor Bible*, vol. 1, page 195). For another, more "civilized" man, would have used the Hebrew word for "eat."

As for cunning and deceit, Jacob seems to have learned them from his mother, who coached him in the deception of his father Isaac into giving his powerful blessing to his younger son Jacob instead of to the older Esau as would have been proper. Jacob then uses this skill in cheating his father-in-law Laban out of his best livestock. Deceit even shows up in Rachel (Jacob's favorite wife of the two) when she steals her father's idols, then lies to him in order to keep them hidden in her saddle.

While it has been noted that all of this maneuvering seems to reside in a family-line that produces the Israelites in general, it also produces Nathanael in whom Jesus sees no guile, along with the Savior Himself (John 1: 47). But if these two brothers represent, not just primitive humans and Israelites, but people of a violent style of life versus more cooperative people, the onus of deceit in this account is on civilization, and is not focussed on the Jews alone. And so the wounded thigh (a universal symbol of impotence) Jacob receives from God in their wrestling surely bears on this. For more on this idea, see the end of the monologue which follows.

The account in Chapter 32 of Jacob wrestling with God is curious. How can any mortal man pit his strength against the Almighty and live to tell of it?

JACOB

MONOLOGUE

A people of strange dignity reside far to the west, of whom the fathers play at wrestling with their sons and bring them so to skills that serve them well when they are men. I presumed this was my dream, for I was not aware, as one will know his hand, that him to whom my father and his father sacrificed, and spoke, discussed at length, and made much of, was no mere ghost, nor goblin for the management of boys.

My father Isaac favored Esau more, my brother born some minutes in advance. He never could abide the close confinement of a tent, but walked the crags, and knew the ways of wolves, and gloried in the pelts of mountain goats. It was my mother took to me. She told me, when my father was about to die, to act my brother outwardly and so be blessed in place of him. I did, and thought it cunning's work of art, that the Lord's hands had moved her hands and mine.

It was alike when Laban put, in place of promised Rachel, Leah of the rheumy eyes. I knew it as a game, a play of wits, and therefore I devised the stripes and spots to reproduce my wealth by thought's manipulation. When Laban and his sons began to scowl, I told my pair of wives the Lord had counseled me to soon remove. It was a shrewd maneuver that would keep my gains.

Now Rachel was the truest twin I had. She knew the idols' import, and she knew as well her father's mind was to retain the flocks and servants that those idols meant. When I became aware of what she'd done, I could not but be pleased. And when her father, knowing of his loss, put on a face to say all was still his, I saw my own deceiving ways in him, and felt approval of both myself and him.

It was soon after that I prayed. For myself and for survival of my house, I grant. And yet I'd witnessed Adonai's swift messengers at tasks and grew to learn He lived. My brother came, four-hundred men with him, all armed, and he as pelted as a goat as always. He'd thought to kill me when I cozened him. Was he thus deadly twenty years along? It seemed perhaps he was. I thought he might have been.

But at the river, where one's life might change, I fell asleep in agony and fear. Immensity of Man fought me in smiles. I landed blows another should have felt, but yet He played my size was his and winced. It would have so continued had He not disabled me by wrenching loose the sinew of my thigh.

And yet I would not let him go, for now I'd come to recognize my father's El Shaddai. I begged his blessing. He transformed my name, my very self, and likewise changed the core of Esau's character, for he turned brotherly, which smoothed the path my twelve sons were to walk. Ah but that limp He gave me figured forth my future illness with more sons. I had but one, my Benjamin, but that occasioned Rachel's death, and in great part my own slow creeping toward my grave.

JACOB

GENESIS 25-35:

19 This is the history of the generations of Isaac, Abraham's son. Abraham became the father of Isaac. 20 Isaac was forty years old when he took Rebekah, the daughter of Bethuel the Syrian of Paddan Aram, the sister of Laban the Syrian, to be his wife. 21 Isaac entreated God for his wife, because she was barren. God was entreated by him, and Rebekah his wife conceived. 22 The children struggled together within her. She said, "If it is like this, why do I live?" She went to inquire of God. 23 God said to her,

"Two nations are in your womb.

Two peoples will be separated from your body.

The one people will be stronger than the other people.

The elder will serve the younger."

24 When her days to be delivered were fulfilled, behold, there were twins in her womb. 25 The first came out red all over, like a hairy garment. They named him Esau. 26 After that, his brother came out, and his hand had hold on Esau's heel. He was named Jacob. Isaac was sixty years old when she bore them.

27 The boys grew. Esau was a skillful hunter, a man of the field. Jacob was a quiet man, living in tents. 28 Now Isaac loved Esau, because he ate his venison. Rebekah loved Jacob. 29 Jacob boiled stew. Esau came in from the field, and he was famished. 30 Esau said to Jacob, "Please feed me with some of that red stew, for I am famished." Therefore his name was called Edom.

31 Jacob said, "First, sell me your birthright."

32 Esau said, "Behold, I am about to die. What good is the birthright to me?"

33 Jacob said, "Swear to me first."

He swore to him. He sold his birthright to Jacob. 34 Jacob gave Esau bread and lentil stew. He ate and drank, rose up, and went his way. So Esau despised his birthright....

27:

1 When Isaac was old, and his eyes were dim, so that he could not see, he called Esau his elder son, and said to him, "My son?"

He said to him, "Here I am."

2 He said, "See now, I am old. I don't know the day of my death. 3 Now therefore, please take your weapons, your quiver and your bow, and go out to the field, and get me venison. 4 Make me savory food, such as I love, and bring it to me, that I may eat, and that my soul may bless you before I die."

5 Rebekah heard when Isaac spoke to Esau his son. Esau went to the field to hunt for venison, and to bring it. 6 Rebekah spoke to Jacob her son, saying, "Behold, I heard your father speak to Esau your brother, saying, 7 'Bring me venison, and make me savory food, that I may eat, and bless you before God before my death.' 8 Now therefore, my son, obey my voice according to that which I command you. 9 Go now to the flock and get me two good young goats from there. I will make them savory food for your father, such as he loves. 10 You shall bring it to your father, that he may eat, so that he may bless you before his death."

11 Jacob said to Rebekah his mother, "Behold, Esau my brother is a hairy man, and I am a smooth man. 12 What if my father touches me? I will seem to him as a deceiver, and I would bring a curse on myself, and not a blessing."

13 His mother said to him, "Let your curse be on me, my son. Only obey my voice, and go get them for me."

14 He went, and got them, and brought them to his mother. His mother made savory food, such as his father loved. 15 Rebekah took the good clothes of Esau, her elder son, which were with her in the house, and put them on Jacob, her younger son. 16 She put the skins of the young goats on his hands, and on the smooth of his neck. 17 She gave the savory food and the bread, which she had prepared, into the hand of her son Jacob.

18 He came to his father, and said, "My father?"

He said, "Here I am. Who are you, my son?"

19 Jacob said to his father, "I am Esau your firstborn. I have done what you asked me to do. Please arise, sit and eat of my venison, that your soul may bless me."

20 Isaac said to his son, "How is it that you have found it so quickly, my son?"

He said, "Because your God gave me success."

21 Isaac said to Jacob, "Please come near, that I may feel you, my son, whether you are really my son Esau or not."

22 Jacob went near to Isaac his father. He felt him, and said, "The voice is Jacob's voice, but the hands are the hands of Esau." 23 He didn't recognize him, because his hands were hairy, like his brother, Esau's hands. So he blessed him. 24 He said, "Are you really my son Esau?"

He said, "I am."

25 He said, "Bring it near to me, and I will eat of my son's venison, that my soul may bless you."

He brought it near to him, and he ate. He brought him wine, and he drank. 26 His father Isaac said to him, "Come near now, and kiss me, my son." 27 He came near, and kissed him. He smelled the smell of his clothing, and blessed him, and said,

"Behold, the smell of my son
is as the smell of a field which God has blessed.
28 God give you of the dew of the sky,
of the fatness of the earth,
and plenty of grain and new wine.
29 Let peoples serve you,
and nations bow down to you.
Be lord over your brothers.
Let your mother's sons bow down to you.
Cursed be everyone who curses you.
Blessed be everyone who blesses you."

30 As soon as Isaac had finished blessing Jacob, and Jacob had just gone out from the presence of Isaac his father, Esau his brother came in from his hunting. 31 He also made savory food, and brought it to his father. He said to his father, "Let my father arise, and eat of his son's venison, that your soul may bless me."

32 Isaac his father said to him, "Who are you?"

He said, "I am your son, your firstborn, Esau."

33 Isaac trembled violently, and said, "Who, then, is he who has taken venison, and brought it me, and I have eaten of all before you came, and have blessed him? Yes, he will be blessed."

34 When Esau heard the words of his father, he cried with an exceedingly great and bitter cry, and said to his father, "Bless me, even me also, my father."

35 He said, "Your brother came with deceit, and has taken away your blessing."

36 He said, "Isn't he rightly named Jacob? For he has supplanted me these two times. He took away my birthright. See, now he has taken away my blessing." He said, "Haven't you reserved a blessing for me?"

37 Isaac answered Esau, "Behold, I have made him your lord, and all his brothers I have given to him for servants. I have sustained him with grain and new wine. What then will I do for you, my son?"

32:

22 He rose up that night, and took his two wives, and his two servants, and his eleven sons, and crossed over the ford of the Jabbok. 23 He took them, and sent them over the stream, and sent over that which he had. 24 Jacob was left alone, and wrestled with a man there until the breaking of the day. 25 When he saw that he didn't prevail against him, the man touched the hollow of his thigh, and the hollow of Jacob's thigh was strained, as he wrestled. 26 The man said, "Let me go, for the day breaks."

Jacob said, "I won't let you go, unless you bless me."

27 He said to him, "What is your name?"

He said, "Jacob".

28 He said, "Your name will no longer be called Jacob, but Israel; for you have fought with God and with men, and have prevailed."

29 Jacob asked him, "Please tell me your name."

He said, "Why is it that you ask what my name is?" He blessed him there.

30 Jacob called the name of the place Peniel: for, he said, "I have seen God face to face, and my life is preserved." 31 The sun rose on him as he passed over Peniel, and he limped because of his thigh. 32 Therefore the children of Israel don't eat the sinew of the hip, which is on the hollow of the thigh, to this day, because he touched the hollow of Jacob's thigh in the sinew of the hip.

CHAPTER 9

Job

■ ■ ■

INTRODUCTION

Reading the book of Job leads many readers to consider our human awareness as severely limited when contrasted with God's vast conceptions, and rightly so. But reading the book is only the beginning if we are to derive the greatest spiritual insights from this gripping book. While every part of the Bible may be read profitably, Job, like the gospels, is in a special class. As a layman, I can approach it only by asking questions about three of its key points:

First, who is in the wrong, Job or God? That is to say, does Job deserve his misery because of his sinfulness, or is God being unfair to Job? Elihu, in his four speeches, says it is Job who is in the wrong, not God—that Job is a sinner. But the reader knows that God considers Job to be "blameless and upright" (Job 1:8).

Second, Elihu says God repays good behavior with prosperity; therefore it follows that Job has sinned. He says, "If [men] obey and serve [God], they will spend the rest of their days in prosperity and their years in contentment. But if they do not listen, they will perish...and die without knowledge" (36:11-12). **Is Elihu correct?**

Third, Job gets his wish when God speaks to him at great length (38-41). One reader will read these passages as a harsh master chastizing a wayward slave, while another will read it in the subdued and kind tones of a wise father correcting his unhappy child. **Which tone suits more the God that Jesus knows?**

JOB

MONOLOGUE

I said, "No more will I consider me ensured against disaster by a contract with Omnipotence. My health dilapidate, my children done away, my body rags, my reputation sick, my peace of mind attacked and ravished." But my brightest pearl that threatened to dissolve was amity with the Lord, for I'd thought obedience, through my awe of him, would surely purchase my prosperity. So when experience insisted otherwise, I thought myself ill treated by the source of good.

Though loyalty to him was my first priority, in my abasement I was forced to hear the lectures of my juniors in the faith. "All is occasioned by your sinfulness." But this precisely was my quandary. I had no rampant sinfulness to halt, for if I did, the halting would resolve my near-complete catastrophe. As it was, I knew no remedy, nowhere to go except the dung heap, my compatriot.

Returning to my healthful fervency appeared pure desperation. I wished a conference with him to state my case. I knew enough of him that I was sure He would surround my argument and win, but where else could I go? I knew these ills came not by chance, but that He lived and would some day set right the gross injustice of the world. But where was this? And how would it occur?

I had a glimpse of something past the grave, but tried to keep it to myself. My friends were men, and men are practical. But in my grief some bits of it escaped my teeth. And then, in time, He came to me— and spoke to me. The Maker and the Ruler of all things had heard my wish and visited the dung heap that was then my fetid home. No mortal king would condescend so low, yet He who made those kings had come to me.

He demonstrated in bewildering detail how blind my vaunted wisdom was, along with that of every man. It was a father's disquisition, not the harsh chastizement of a tyrant's rant. When I had seen his vastness face-to-face, I saw at once my littleness and, shamed, I asked forgiveness.

This was, it seems, the key I never thought to wish were mine. I would be most content, were He to let me keep my scabs and petty lecturers until my death.

JOB

JOB 1:

1 There was a man in the land of Uz, whose name was Job. That man was blameless and upright, and one who feared God, and turned away from evil. 2 There were born to him seven sons and three daughters. 3 His possessions also were seven thousand sheep, three thousand camels, five hundred yoke of oxen, five hundred female donkeys, and a very great household; so that this man was the greatest of all the children of the east. 4 His sons went and held a feast in the house of each one on his birthday; and they sent and called for their three sisters to eat and to drink with them. 5 It was so, when the days of their feasting had run their course, that Job sent and sanctified them, and rose up early in the morning, and offered burnt offerings according to the number of them all. For Job said, "It may be that my sons have sinned, and renounced God in their hearts." Job did so continually.

6 Now on the day when God's sons came to present themselves before God, Satan also came among them. 7 God said to Satan, "Where have you come from?"

Then Satan answered God, and said, "From going back and forth in the earth, and from walking up and down in it."

8 God said to Satan, "Have you considered my servant, Job? For there is no one like him in the earth, a blameless and an upright man, one who fears God, and turns away from evil."

9 Then Satan answered God, and said, "Does Job fear God for nothing? 10 Haven't you made a hedge around him, and around his house, and around all that he has, on every side? You have blessed the work of his hands, and his substance is increased in the land. 11 But stretch out

your hand now, and touch all that he has, and he will renounce you to your face."

12 God said to Satan, "Behold, all that he has is in your power. Only on himself don't stretch out your hand."

So Satan went out from the presence of God. 13 It fell on a day when his sons and his daughters were eating and drinking wine in their oldest brother's house, 14 that there came a messenger to Job, and said, "The oxen were plowing, and the donkeys feeding beside them, 15 and the Sabeans attacked, and took them away. Yes, they have killed the servants with the edge of the sword, and I alone have escaped to tell you."

16 While he was still speaking, there also came another, and said, "The fire of God has fallen from the sky, and has burned up the sheep and the servants, and consumed them, and I alone have escaped to tell you."

17 While he was still speaking, there came also another, and said, "The Chaldeans made three bands, and swept down on the camels, and have taken them away, yes, and killed the servants with the edge of the sword; and I alone have escaped to tell you."

18 While he was still speaking, there came also another, and said, "Your sons and your daughters were eating and drinking wine in their oldest brother's house, 19 and behold, there came a great wind from the wilderness, and struck the four corners of the house, and it fell on the young men, and they are dead. I alone have escaped to tell you."

20 Then Job arose, and tore his robe, and shaved his head, and fell down on the ground, and worshiped. 21 He said, "Naked I came out of my mother's womb, and naked shall I return there. God gave, and God has taken away. Blessed be God's name." 22 In all this, Job didn't sin, nor charge God with wrongdoing.

36:

1 Elihu also continued, and said,

2 "Bear with me a little, and I will show you;
for I still have something to say on God's behalf.

3 I will get my knowledge from afar,
and will ascribe righteousness to my Maker.
4 For truly my words are not false.
One who is perfect in knowledge is with you.
5 "Behold, God is mighty, and doesn't despise anyone.
He is mighty in strength of understanding.
6 He doesn't preserve the life of the wicked,
but gives to the afflicted their right.
7 He doesn't withdraw his eyes from the righteous,
but with kings on the throne,
he sets them forever, and they are exalted.
8 If they are bound in fetters,
and are taken in the cords of afflictions,
9 then he shows them their work,
and their transgressions, that they have behaved themselves proudly.
10 He also opens their ears to instruction,
and commands that they return from iniquity.
11 If they listen and serve him,
they shall spend their days in prosperity,
and their years in pleasures.
12 But if they don't listen, they shall perish by the sword;
they shall die without knowledge.

13 "But those who are godless in heart lay up anger.
They don't cry for help when he binds them.
14 They die in youth.
Their life perishes among the unclean.
15 He delivers the afflicted by their affliction,
and opens their ear in oppression.
16 Yes, he would have allured you out of distress,
into a wide place, where there is no restriction.
That which is set on your table would be full of fatness.

17 "But you are full of the judgment of the wicked.
  Judgment and justice take hold of you.
  18 Don't let riches entice you to wrath,
  neither let the great size of a bribe turn you aside.
  19 Would your wealth sustain you in distress,
  or all the might of your strength?
  20 Don't desire the night,
  when people are cut off in their place.
  21 Take heed, don't regard iniquity;
  for you have chosen this rather than affliction.
  22 Behold, God is exalted in his power.
  Who is a teacher like him?
  23 Who has prescribed his way for him?
  Or who can say, 'You have committed unrighteousness?'

24 "Remember that you magnify his work,
  whereof men have sung.
  25 All men have looked on it.
  Man sees it afar off.
  26 Behold, God is great, and we don't know him.
  The number of his years is unsearchable.
  27 For he draws up the drops of water,
  which distill in rain from his vapor,
  28 Which the skies pour down
  and which drop on man abundantly.
  29 Yes, can any understand the spreading of the clouds,
  and the thunderings of his pavilion?
  30 Behold, he spreads his light around him.
  He covers the bottom of the sea.
  31 For by these he judges the people.
  He gives food in abundance.
  32 He covers his hands with the lightning,
  and commands it to strike the mark.

33 Its noise tells about him,
and the livestock also concerning the storm that comes up.

38:

1 Then God answered Job out of the whirlwind,
2 "Who is this who darkens counsel
by words without knowledge?
3 Brace yourself like a man,
for I will question you, then you answer me!

4 "Where were you when I laid the foundations of the earth?
Declare, if you have understanding.
5 Who determined its measures, if you know?
Or who stretched the line on it?
6 Whereupon were its foundations fastened?
Or who laid its cornerstone,
7 when the morning stars sang together,
and all the sons of God shouted for joy?

8 "Or who shut up the sea with doors,
when it broke out of the womb,
9 when I made clouds its garment,
and wrapped it in thick darkness,
10 marked out for it my bound,
set bars and doors,
11 and said, 'Here you may come, but no further.
Here your proud waves shall be stayed?'

12 "Have you commanded the morning in your days,
and caused the dawn to know its place;
13 that it might take hold of the ends of the earth,
and shake the wicked out of it?
14 It is changed as clay under the seal,

and presented as a garment.
15 From the wicked, their light is withheld.
The high arm is broken.

16 "Have you entered into the springs of the sea?
　Or have you walked in the recesses of the deep?
　17 Have the gates of death been revealed to you?
　Or have you seen the gates of the shadow of death?
　18 Have you comprehended the earth in its width?
　Declare, if you know it all.

19 "What is the way to the dwelling of light?
　As for darkness, where is its place,
　20 that you should take it to its bound,
　that you should discern the paths to its house?
　21 Surely you know, for you were born then,
　and the number of your days is great!
　22 Have you entered the treasuries of the snow,
　or have you seen the treasures of the hail,
　23 which I have reserved against the time of trouble,
　against the day of battle and war?
　24 By what way is the lightning distributed,
　or the east wind scattered on the earth?

25 Who has cut a channel for the flood water,
　or the path for the thunderstorm;
　26 To cause it to rain on a land where no man is;
　on the wilderness, in which there is no man;
　27 to satisfy the waste and desolate ground,
　to cause the tender grass to grow?
　28 Does the rain have a father?
　Or who fathers the drops of dew?
　29 Out of whose womb came the ice?

The gray frost of the sky, who has given birth to it?
30 The waters become hard like stone,
when the surface of the deep is frozen.

31 "Can you bind the cluster of the Pleiades,
or loosen the cords of Orion?
32 Can you lead the constellations out in their season?
Or can you guide the Bear with her cubs?
33 Do you know the laws of the heavens?
Can you establish its dominion over the earth?

34 "Can you lift up your voice to the clouds,
That abundance of waters may cover you?
35 Can you send out lightnings, that they may go?
Do they report to you, 'Here we are?'
36 Who has put wisdom in the inward parts?
Or who has given understanding to the mind?
37 Who can count the clouds by wisdom?
Or who can pour out the containers of the sky,
38 when the dust runs into a mass,
and the clods of earth stick together?

39 "Can you hunt the prey for the lioness,
or satisfy the appetite of the young lions,
40 when they crouch in their dens,
and lie in wait in the thicket?
41 Who provides for the raven his prey,
when his young ones cry to God,
and wander for lack of food?

42:

1 Then Job answered God,
2 "I know that you can do all things,

and that no purpose of yours can be restrained.
3 You asked, 'Who is this who hides counsel without knowledge?'
therefore I have uttered that which I didn't understand,
things too wonderful for me, which I didn't know.
4 You said, 'Listen, now, and I will speak;
I will question you, and you will answer me.'
5 I had heard of you by the hearing of the ear,
but now my eye sees you.
6 Therefore I abhor myself,
and repent in dust and ashes."

7 It was so, that after God had spoken these words to Job, God said to Eliphaz the Temanite, "My wrath is kindled against you, and against your two friends; for you have not spoken of me the thing that is right, as my servant Job has. 8 Now therefore, take to yourselves seven bulls and seven rams, and go to my servant Job, and offer up for yourselves a burnt offering; and my servant Job shall pray for you, for I will accept him, that I not deal with you according to your folly. For you have not spoken of me the thing that is right, as my servant Job has."

9 So Eliphaz the Temanite and Bildad the Shuhite and Zophar the Naamathite went, and did what God commanded them, and God accepted Job.

10 God turned the captivity of Job, when he prayed for his friends. God gave Job twice as much as he had before. 11 Then came there to him all his brothers, and all his sisters, and all those who had been of his acquaintance before, and ate bread with him in his house. They comforted him, and consoled him concerning all the evil that God had brought on him. Everyone also gave him a piece of money, and everyone a ring of gold.

12 So God blessed the latter end of Job more than his beginning. He had fourteen thousand sheep, six thousand camels, one thousand yoke of oxen, and a thousand female donkeys. 13 He had also seven

sons and three daughters. 14 He called the name of the first, Jemimah; and the name of the second, Keziah; and the name of the third, Keren Happuch. 15 In all the land were no women found so beautiful as the daughters of Job. Their father gave them an inheritance among their brothers. 16 After this Job lived one hundred forty years, and saw his sons, and his sons' sons, to four generations. 17 So Job died, being old and full of days.

JONAH

CHAPTER 10

Jonah

■ ■ ■

INTRODUCTION

In spite of Isaiah's revelation of Judaism's great challenge from God—"I will also make you a light to the Gentiles, that you may bring my salvation to the ends of the earth"—there was a strong streak of exclusivism that persisted (Isaiah 49:6b). Gentiles were normally seen as outside the blessings and privileges of God's chosen people. The reasons given for this prejudice ranged from contact with pork, through mixing materials in woven cloth, to not being descended from Abraham.

The story of Jonah seems to personify this attitude in the extreme. He sees the Ninevites as being so sinful that they are without hope of repentance and God's forgiveness. Also, though a prophet and apparently an intimate acquaintance of God, he is so mired in this judgment that, when he is forced into preaching to Ninevah, and the people repent as a result of his preaching, Jonah is angry and blames God for being too soft on them. In his view, they should never have been allowed to repent.

The result is a book of extreme actions and reactions. So exaggerated is it in fact that it combines a serious lesson with a somewhat comic tone. What, for example, do you make of Jonah's trying to escape the notice of the creator of the universe by means of a short voyage to Tarshish? Or consider his extreme anger over a mere vine that God provided and then withered.

JONAH

MONOLOGUE

I plopped me down, bedraggled, failed and pooped with preaching to an earless mob. The day was hot. A fig tree shaded me. Just drifting off when, "BIRD" He shouts and breaks my nap and eardrums all in one. It is his nickname for myself (I'm Dove) for being hesitant to plow the sand. "Scoot off to Ninevah," He thunders on (or words to that effect), "that monstrous burg, and tickle ears with this: I know their tricks."

Oh Ninevah, says I to me, the town that crawls with hookers and their ruttish queen. When halfway decent Jews told me, "Get lost," my first reaction should have been, "Aha, why not Ninevah? They worship god (wrong one, of course). Smooth sailing all the way." Good luck on his new enterprise, I thought, and hopped a tub in Joppa that was aimed at Tarshish, just as far from Ninevah and his great larynx as a ship can sail.

But oh, the ocean. I had thought it flat. It turned that day to perpendicular. The scow was buckling, so the gobs began to yell for different gods, their favorites: Ahura Mazda, Baal, Poseidon. I was below, continuing my nap and breathing in the perfume of the bilge, but I could tell their empty prayers had failed. So then I heard the splashes as they dumped their lading overboard. That failed as well, and down the boatswain came to throw me too, or so I thought. It happened that he said to get to praying to my God. Yes, right, thought I. I pay this swabbie to transport my carcass miles away from the One's voice, and presto! he says ask for the One's voice.

But things were frantic. He went off saying that they had to find the skulking guilty guy who was aboard and causing all the fuss. They had to draw the lots. And, true to form, the lots said me. I got the third degree. They recognized my scheme, so I said, "Me." They weren't the swiftest boys to catch a thought, so I gave it another word or two: "You threw the rest of it. Now throw me in." But all that got was funny looks, as if I'd come out here because I liked to drown.

But rowing hard for shore (their next device) proved just as futile as the rest, so then they prayed to the Lord to forgive them for deep-sixing me. I sailed (this time without a deck to touch my feet) beyond the rail and made another splash, and sank below their voices and below the world of bread, below the light. I hadn't thought the dead would own such popping eyes. They stared at me descending like a wounded bird, as if I had disturbed some protocol. The dark enveloped me and I was dead. But (shall I say it?) I was glad to be so taken off. It meant I was beyond his call, his reach, his chores that never worked.

But ah, the dark! I'd sought oblivion. I got instead solidity of loss. Here was no sense, no up or down, no straight. There seemed no bottom to abhorrences. The teeth surrounded me, annihilated all I was, disposed me farther from the everyday comestibles of life with Adonai's and the world of sense He gave. I prayed. He heard. I cast up on the shore.

I was where I'd started. Then the Voice: "Get up, you avian recalcitrance." Caught resting once again. And so I went.

I got to Ninevah, a stinking dump. I found a corner, went through my routine, the forty days of leniency, the threat. It tumbled from my mouth. I hardly heard the words myself, so useless did it seem, so misdirected to a mound of muck.

I should have known; the hardest heads of all, the lushes, lechers, whores, the murderers, whose conscience never twinged to rob the sick or hold the wages of an honest man, these, *these* repented. These turned sweet at once. I'd thought their ears were fortresses. Instead, their resistance dropped like ripened figs, and just as sweet in Adonai's mouth. It was as usual: He's tender and compassionate. It takes an eon for his anger to build up. And all it takes to bring it down is stopping what you've done and giving in. I told Him so. I'd had enough of it. I also said I'd had enough of life.

I went off where the morning sun shone on the city's filth and made myself a shade, a gimcrack shelter where I sat and watched to see if He would raze that pile of trash. But nothing happened to the town. It was *my* hair He twitched again; a castor bean took root and filled the hole the sun looked through. I almost laughed. Now this was more my style.

It lasted just one day. The following, it withered, and my anger heated up. Was I his bird? Would I have treated birds the way He scorched his prophet's balding skull? I ground my teeth. I clenched my fists and growled.

And then like purling water He spoke soft: "Upset by nothing more than this? A plant you never planted, one that lives one day? And why should I not grieve for Ninevah, this city of a hundred thousand souls?"

JONAH

JONAH 1:

1 Now God's word came to Jonah the son of Amittai, saying, 2 "Arise, go to Nineveh, that great city, and preach against it, for their wickedness has come up before me."

3 But Jonah rose up to flee to Tarshish from the presence of God. He went down to Joppa, and found a ship going to Tarshish; so he paid its fare, and went down into it, to go with them to Tarshish from the presence of God. 4 But God sent out a great wind on the sea, and there was a mighty storm on the sea, so that the ship was likely to break up. 5 Then the mariners were afraid, and every man cried to his god. They threw the cargo that was in the ship into the sea to lighten the ship. But Jonah had gone down into the innermost parts of the ship, and he was laying down, and was fast asleep. 6 So the ship master came to him, and said to him, "What do you mean, sleeper? Arise, call on your God! Maybe your God will notice us, so that we won't perish."

7 They all said to each other, "Come! Let's cast lots, that we may know who is responsible for this evil that is on us." So they cast lots, and the lot fell on Jonah. 8 Then they asked him, "Tell us, please, for whose

cause this evil is on us. What is your occupation? Where do you come from? What is your country? Of what people are you?"

9 He said to them, "I am a Hebrew, and I fear God, the God of heaven, who has made the sea and the dry land."

10 Then the men were exceedingly afraid, and said to him, "What have you done?" For the men knew that he was fleeing from the presence of God, because he had told them. 11 Then they said to him, "What shall we do to you, that the sea may be calm to us?" For the sea grew more and more stormy. 12 He said to them, "Take me up, and throw me into the sea. Then the sea will be calm for you; for I know that because of me this great storm is on you."

13 Nevertheless the men rowed hard to get them back to the land; but they could not, for the sea grew more and more stormy against them. 14 Therefore they cried to God, and said, "We beg you, God, we beg you, don't let us die for this man's life, and don't lay on us innocent blood; for you, God, have done as it pleased you." 15 So they took up Jonah, and threw him into the sea; and the sea ceased its raging. 16 Then the men feared God exceedingly; and they offered a sacrifice to God, and made vows.

17 God prepared a great fish to swallow up Jonah, and Jonah was in the belly of the fish three days and three nights.

4:

1 But it displeased Jonah exceedingly, and he was angry. 2 He prayed to God, and said, "Please, God, wasn't this what I said when I was still in my own country? Therefore I hurried to flee to Tarshish, for I knew that you are a gracious God, and merciful, slow to anger, and abundant in loving kindness, and you relent of doing harm. 3 Therefore now, God, take, I beg you, my life from me; for it is better for me to die than to live."

4 God said, "Is it right for you to be angry?"

5 Then Jonah went out of the city, and sat on the east side of the city, and there made himself a booth, and sat under it in the shade, until he

might see what would become of the city. 6 God God prepared a vine, and made it to come up over Jonah, that it might be a shade over his head, to deliver him from his discomfort. So Jonah was exceedingly glad because of the vine. 7 But God prepared a worm at dawn the next day, and it chewed on the vine, so that it withered. 8 When the sun arose, God prepared a sultry east wind; and the sun beat on Jonah's head, so that he fainted, and requested for himself that he might die, and said, "It is better for me to die than to live."

9 God said to Jonah, "Is it right for you to be angry about the vine?" He said, "I am right to be angry, even to death."

10 God said, "You have been concerned for the vine, for which you have not labored, neither made it grow; which came up in a night, and perished in a night. 11 Shouldn't I be concerned for Nineveh, that great city, in which are more than one hundred twenty thousand persons who can't discern between their right hand and their left hand; and also much livestock?"

JOSEPH

CHAPTER 11

Joseph and His Brothers

■ ■ ■

INTRODUCTION

There is no more moving act of forgiveness in the Old Testament than Joseph's forgiveness of his brothers for having sold him into slavery. Of course Joseph had not displayed wisdom in telling them his dreams of his becoming their master, but then he was, at the time, only seventeen years old (Genesis 37:5-11). It may be that Joseph remembers his youthful indiscretions when forgiving his brothers, though we are not told that he does.

What we are told is that he looks back over the twenty-two years since they sold him, and he sees a pattern in the history of their interaction. Even the earliest speakers of Hebrew were natural and accomplished historians. This was no doubt caused by their religion's being bound up with a historical perspective in remembering a past filled with God's interactions with them. It was therefore natural for Joseph, and for the writer(s) of Genesis, to take this historical view, even if only the history of one (admittedly important) family.

And the pattern that Joseph sees is encapsulated in what he tells his brothers after revealing his identity to them: "Do not be distressed and do not be angry with yourselves for selling me here, because it was to save lives that God sent me ahead of you" (45:5). He then allots to them a fertile area called Goshen, where they can live in peace and plenty away from the prejudices of the native Egyptian people.

JOSEPH AND HIS BROTHERS

MONOLOGUE

The Lord raised me up from stripling nuisance to be steward of the greatest earthly strength. My brothers' perfidy was still beneath the floor of memory, but now my floor was polished stone, and I was supplicated by both general and prince. It was my one, my inner task to daily prune the tree of self-delight that roots in power's soil.

In my slavery, when I was Potiphar's and given charge of all he owned, but with his wife apart, the household servanthood would hiss about her rank adulteries. She was of tender age, while he had reached the years of withered legs. It seems he guessed her ways but had no face for the attendant smirking of his house. Her suitors all I sent away, as thinking Potiphar would have it so. But then it was that I alone remained to be the object of her turning eye.

Yet gratitude and self-restraint are not a guarantee of peace beneath the sun. It is on high alone such righteousness is noted in detail and not forgot. It was the One on High observing all, with here and there a dream from him, would harmonize those culminating days when I could teach compassion to my kin. My brothers' pride of eldership had led them to strike down in grief my father's hope, these brothers whom I had in callowness imagined that my dreams would bring them joy.

Now that they came to my transfigured state as Pharaoh's high vizier, I had two tasks: to tame their arrogance, and keep my own pride in constraint while curbing theirs. Impossible to do had I not seen the hand of the Lord in our roles' exchange, I held that shaping vision for my life.

At last He brought me Benjamin, the boy who lived my absent youth. Then father Israel, my future in my gray and wrinkled age. I wept for them and for myself in them. I wept that we had lost the years between. But something here was salvaged. I would not stay blind with tears until they carted me into the tomb. My sons would know their house in all its jollity and fractured love. And what our loss produced was better than what might have been at home. And the Lord knew it all.

JOSEPH AND HIS BROTHERS

GENESIS 37:

2 This is the history of the generations of Jacob. Joseph, being seventeen years old, was feeding the flock with his brothers. He was a boy with the sons of Bilhah and Zilpah, his father's wives. Joseph brought an evil report of them to their father. 3 Now Israel loved Joseph more than all his children, because he was the son of his old age, and he made him a tunic of many colors. 4 His brothers saw that their father loved him more than all his brothers, and they hated him, and couldn't speak peaceably to him.

5 Joseph dreamed a dream, and he told it to his brothers, and they hated him all the more. 6 He said to them, "Please hear this dream which I have dreamed: 7 for behold, we were binding sheaves in the field, and behold, my sheaf arose and also stood upright; and behold, your sheaves came around, and bowed down to my sheaf."

8 His brothers asked him, "Will you indeed reign over us? Will you indeed have dominion over us?" They hated him all the more for his dreams and for his words. 9 He dreamed yet another dream, and told it to his brothers, and said, "Behold, I have dreamed yet another dream: and behold, the sun and the moon and eleven stars bowed down to me." 10 He told it to his father and to his brothers. His father rebuked him, and said to him, "What is this dream that you have dreamed? Will I and your mother and your brothers indeed come to bow ourselves down to you to the earth?" 11 His brothers envied him, but his father kept this saying in mind.

12 His brothers went to feed their father's flock in Shechem. 13 Israel said to Joseph, "Aren't your brothers feeding the flock in Shechem? Come, and I will send you to them." He said to him, "Here I am."

14 He said to him, "Go now, see whether it is well with your brothers, and well with the flock; and bring me word again." So he sent him out of the valley of Hebron, and he came to Shechem. 15 A certain man found him, and behold, he was wandering in the field. The man asked him, "What are you looking for?"

16 He said, "I am looking for my brothers. Tell me, please, where they are feeding the flock."

17 The man said, "They have left here, for I heard them say, 'Let's go to Dothan.'"

Joseph went after his brothers, and found them in Dothan. 18 They saw him afar off, and before he came near to them, they conspired against him to kill him. 19 They said to one another, "Behold, this dreamer comes. 20 Come now therefore, and let's kill him, and cast him into one of the pits, and we will say, 'An evil animal has devoured him.' We will see what will become of his dreams."

21 Reuben heard it, and delivered him out of their hand, and said, "Let's not take his life." 22 Reuben said to them, "Shed no blood. Throw him into this pit that is in the wilderness, but lay no hand on him"—that he might deliver him out of their hand, to restore him to his father. 23 When Joseph came to his brothers, they stripped Joseph of his tunic, the tunic of many colors that was on him; 24 and they took him, and threw him into the pit. The pit was empty. There was no water in it.

25 They sat down to eat bread, and they lifted up their eyes and looked, and saw a caravan of Ishmaelites was coming from Gilead, with their camels bearing spices and balm and myrrh, going to carry it down to Egypt. 26 Judah said to his brothers, "What profit is it if we kill our brother and conceal his blood? 27 Come, and let's sell him to the Ishmaelites, and not let our hand be on him; for he is our brother, our flesh." His brothers listened to him. 28 Midianites who were merchants

passed by, and they drew and lifted up Joseph out of the pit, and sold Joseph to the Ishmaelites for twenty pieces of silver. The merchants brought Joseph into Egypt.

29 Reuben returned to the pit, and saw that Joseph wasn't in the pit; and he tore his clothes. 30 He returned to his brothers, and said, "The child is no more; and I, where will I go?" 31 They took Joseph's tunic, and killed a male goat, and dipped the tunic in the blood. 32 They took the tunic of many colors, and they brought it to their father, and said, "We have found this. Examine it, now, and see if it is your son's tunic or not."

33 He recognized it, and said, "It is my son's tunic. An evil animal has devoured him. Joseph is without doubt torn in pieces." 34 Jacob tore his clothes, and put sackcloth on his waist, and mourned for his son many days. 35 All his sons and all his daughters rose up to comfort him, but he refused to be comforted. He said, "For I will go down to Sheol to my son, mourning." His father wept for him. 36 The Midianites sold him into Egypt to Potiphar, an officer of Pharaoh's, the captain of the guard.

45:

1 Then Joseph couldn't control himself before all those who stood before him, and he called out, "Cause everyone to go out from me!" No one else stood with him, while Joseph made himself known to his brothers. 2 He wept aloud. The Egyptians heard, and the house of Pharaoh heard. 3 Joseph said to his brothers, "I am Joseph! Does my father still live?"

His brothers couldn't answer him; for they were terrified at his presence. 4 Joseph said to his brothers, "Come near to me, please."

They came near. He said,"I am Joseph, your brother, whom you sold into Egypt. 5 Now don't be grieved, nor angry with yourselves, that you sold me here, for God sent me before you to preserve life. 6 For these two years the famine has been in the land, and there are yet five years, in which there will be no plowing and no harvest. 7 God sent me before you to preserve for you a remnant in the earth, and to save you alive by a great deliverance. 8 So now it wasn't you who sent me here, but God, and he has made me a father to Pharaoh, lord of all his house, and ruler over all the land of Egypt. 9 Hurry, and go up to my father, and tell him, 'This is what your son Joseph says, "God has made me lord of all Egypt. Come down to me. Don't wait. 10 You shall dwell in the land of Goshen, and you will be near to me, you, your children, your children's children, your flocks, your herds, and all that you have. 11 There I will provide for you; for there are yet five years of famine; lest you come to poverty, you, and your household, and all that you have." ' 12 Behold, your eyes see, and the eyes of my brother Benjamin, that it is my mouth that speaks to you. 13 You shall tell my father of all my glory in Egypt, and of all that you have seen. You shall hurry and bring my father down here." 14 He fell on his brother Benjamin's neck, and wept, and Benjamin wept on his neck. 15 He kissed all his brothers, and wept on them. After that his brothers talked with him.

16 The report of it was heard in Pharaoh's house, saying, "Joseph's brothers have come." It pleased Pharaoh well, and his servants. 17 Pharaoh said to Joseph, "Tell your brothers, 'Do this: Load your animals, and go, travel to the land of Canaan. 18 Take your father and your households, and come to me, and I will give you the good of the land of Egypt, and you will eat the fat of the land.' 19 Now you are commanded to do this: Take wagons out of the land of Egypt for your little ones, and for your wives, and bring your father, and come. 20 Also, don't concern yourselves about your belongings, for the good of all the land of Egypt is yours."

21 The sons of Israel did so. Joseph gave them wagons, according to the commandment of Pharaoh, and gave them provision for the way. 22 He gave each one of them changes of clothing, but to Benjamin he gave three hundred pieces of silver and five changes of clothing. 23 He sent the following to his father: ten donkeys loaded with the good things of

Egypt, and ten female donkeys loaded with grain and bread and provision for his father by the way. 24 So he sent his brothers away, and they departed. He said to them, "See that you don't quarrel on the way."

25 They went up out of Egypt, and came into the land of Canaan, to Jacob their father. 26 They told him, saying, "Joseph is still alive, and he is ruler over all the land of Egypt." His heart fainted, for he didn't believe them. 27 They told him all the words of Joseph, which he had said to them. When he saw the wagons which Joseph had sent to carry him, the spirit of Jacob, their father, revived. 28 Israel said, "It is enough. Joseph my son is still alive. I will go and see him before I die."

JUDAS

CHAPTER 12

Judas Iscariot

■ ■ ■

INTRODUCTION

Judas Iscariot is a puzzlement for those of us who would like to know his motivation for betraying Jesus. The Lord picked him to be one of the twelve apostles, sent him with the others to heal and preach, and entrusted him with the apostles' combined collection of funds. Jesus even mentions the apostasy of Judas in his prayer for his disciples, acknowledging that one of the twelve given him by the Father was lost "in accordance with the scriptures" (John 17:12).

But it is not clear in any of the gospels what exactly was the reason for Judas' betrayal. All that's clear is that Judas was not lost beyond hope until he had accepted bread and wine from Jesus' own hand while planning the betrayal (John 13:27). The great probability is that Jesus keeps Judas with him while there is some hope that he will repent, but when the Passover arrives and it is time for Jesus to die, He offers communion to his betrayer, senses that the man's mind is on betrayal while he eats and drinks, and knows that Satan enters him at that moment. (This alone should caution us all about the mind-set with which we take communion.)

Was Judas' primary motivation money? Ambition? Lack of true belief? Was he, as some think, a radical revolutionary who was disappointed by Jesus' going to his humiliating death without a physical fight?

JUDAS ISCARIOT

MONOLOGUE

You ask me for the pattern of my life. And why would you do so? You wish to set a trap for me, to have me list my reasons for betraying Him. And why? I think I see it there behind your back. You desire an incomplete account that misses the mark of your own sins. That would indicate you are no Judas Iscariot.

Well I will give you no such list. Oh yes, I took my little morsels from the moneybag, but that was to support my elder age when the eleven would not speak to me. Likewise the thirty bits of silver. None of it would be the treasure of a wealthy man. And is not filching much alike with begging? A pot of porridge both?

And what then of ambition? You are not serious in asking this, I'm sure. What heights could I attain to with my reputation gone, the sole addition that puts mankind above the dog. Do me the favor of more likely accusations.

Ah now you come more near reality, and yet amiss as well—my disbelief. In what, pray tell? In his messiahship? I must protest, for when the bumbling Peter blurted this the rabbi's title, did I deny his fawning compliment? I did not, and by my judicious silence I agreed He was anointed king.

What else have you for trapping me? My politics? What is so wrong with wanting the Lord's kingdom on my span of life? Was Moses nudely nailed upon a cross to free the tribes? Of course not. He had his dignity. So why this common Galilean in his place? Faugh, it bankrupts reason.

JUDAS ISCARIOT

MATTHEW 26:

14 Then one of the twelve, who was called Judas Iscariot, went to the chief priests, 15 and said, "What are you willing to give me, that I should

deliver him to you?" They weighed out for him thirty pieces of silver. 16
From that time he sought opportunity to betray him....

20 Now when evening had come, he was reclining at the table with
the twelve disciples. 21 As they were eating, he said, "Most certainly I
tell you that one of you will betray me."

22 They were exceedingly sorrowful, and each began to ask him, "It
isn't me, is it, Lord?"

23 He answered, "He who dipped his hand with me in the dish will
betray me. 24 The Son of Man goes, even as it is written of him, but
woe to that man through whom the Son of Man is betrayed! It would
be better for that man if he had not been born."

25 Judas, who betrayed him, answered, "It isn't me, is it, Rabbi?"
He said to him, "You said it."

JOHN 13:

18 I don't speak concerning all of you. I know whom I have chosen.
But that the Scripture may be fulfilled, 'He who eats bread with me
has lifted up his heel against me.' 19 From now on, I tell you before it
happens, that when it happens, you may believe that I am he. 20 Most
certainly I tell you, he who receives whomever I send, receives me; and
he who receives me, receives him who sent me."

21 When Jesus had said this, he was troubled in spirit, and testified,
"Most certainly I tell you that one of you will betray me."

22 The disciples looked at one another, perplexed about whom he
spoke. 23 One of his disciples, whom Jesus loved, was at the table, leaning against Jesus' breast. 24 Simon Peter therefore beckoned to him, and
said to him, "Tell us who it is of whom he speaks."

25 He, leaning back, as he was, on Jesus' breast, asked him, "Lord,
who is it?"

26 Jesus therefore answered, "It is he to whom I will give this piece
of bread when I have dipped it." So when he had dipped the piece of
bread, he gave it to Judas, the son of Simon Iscariot. 27 After the piece
of bread, then Satan entered into him.

Then Jesus said to him, "What you do, do quickly."

28 Now no man at the table knew why he said this to him. 29 For some thought, because Judas had the money box, that Jesus said to him, "Buy what things we need for the feast," or that he should give something to the poor. 30 Therefore having received that morsel, he went out immediately. It was night.

17:

12 While I was with them in the world, I kept them in your name. I have kept those whom you have given me. None of them is lost except the son of destruction, that the Scripture might be fulfilled.

LAZARUS

CHAPTER 13

Lazarus

■ ■ ■

INTRODUCTION

Have you ever noticed that the advertisers' photographs of fast food—hamburgers, for instance—always look much more appealing than the real thing when it is handed to you? It can be something of a let-down, like so many temptations that are over-sold. In this fallen world, we are constantly grasping at sensations, only to find that they are, when compared with the promise, disappointing.

But God's promises are not over-sold or disappointing. Consider Jesus' first miracle when the *better* wine came last (much to the surprise of the wedding headwaiter). Rather than the typical order at such feasts, Jesus' miraculous wine was remarkably more delicious than what had preceded it.

In a similar way, the raising of Lazarus, while pointing forward like a promise to Jesus' Resurrection, is not a resurrection in the full sense of the word. Lazarus was revived, brought back to life only to one day die again, whereas Jesus was resurrected to a *new* life that was no longer vulnerable to the threat of death. Both came back to life, but Lazarus came back to his old life in order to add to God's glory, while Jesus' Resurrection started a world religion.

And yet in addition to all these considerations, it probably was not a joyful experience for Lazarus, but rather some sort of holding period that prevented his body's decay and the smell that Martha had mistakenly expected. And that probability, along with Jesus' weeping, is what the following monologue focuses on.

How would you have reacted to having been raised from death as Lazarus was?

LAZARUS

MONOLOGUE

I did nothing remarkable in my life but die— sicken and die. I lay on my bed, my life leaking out of me, asking, begging for the rabbi to come and pull the pest through his hands and into...into what? Oblivion? I don't know. But what He'd done for others, for me, his friend, He put aside perhaps. Then things took on a haze: the lamp, the walls, my sisters' faces—I lost track of everything.

I said I died. I should be careful what I say. When I stopped breathing and went cool, someone must have wrapped my body, slid me in a cave, and rolled a stone across the opening. They *must* have done so; that's where I shuffled out when I was called.

It was as though I slept. Some things I heard, and something in me translated them to dreams. I saw no seraphim, felt no burst of sudden joy, nothing that the Pharisees had taught. Only rest, a pallid sense of being shelved.

And then I heard a voice I knew, the rabbi's voice, say, "Lazarus, come out." It was like the sound of four hundred voices singing psalms of ascent, or morning light upon my eyelids. That's when I felt the linen bindings that encircled me.

My sister later told me He had wept for me. I love that man.

LAZARUS

JOHN 11:

1 Now a certain man was sick, Lazarus from Bethany, of the village of Mary and her sister, Martha. 2 It was that Mary who had anointed the Lord with ointment and wiped his feet with her hair, whose brother, Lazarus, was sick. 3 The sisters therefore sent to him, saying, "Lord,

behold, he for whom you have great affection is sick." 4 But when Jesus heard it, he said, "This sickness is not to death, but for the glory of God, that God's Son may be glorified by it." 5 Now Jesus loved Martha, and her sister, and Lazarus. 6 When therefore he heard that he was sick, he stayed two days in the place where he was. 7 Then after this he said to the disciples, "Let's go into Judea again."

8 The disciples asked him, "Rabbi, the Jews were just trying to stone you. Are you going there again?"

9 Jesus answered, "Aren't there twelve hours of daylight? If a man walks in the day, he doesn't stumble, because he sees the light of this world. 10 But if a man walks in the night, he stumbles, because the light isn't in him." 11 He said these things, and after that, he said to them, "Our friend, Lazarus, has fallen asleep, but I am going so that I may awake him out of sleep."

12 The disciples therefore said, "Lord, if he has fallen asleep, he will recover."

13 Now Jesus had spoken of his death, but they thought that he spoke of taking rest in sleep. 14 So Jesus said to them plainly then, "Lazarus is dead. 15 I am glad for your sakes that I was not there, so that you may believe. Nevertheless, let's go to him."

16 Thomas therefore, who is called Didymus, said to his fellow disciples, "Let's go also, that we may die with him."

17 So when Jesus came, he found that he had been in the tomb four days already. 18 Now Bethany was near Jerusalem, about fifteen stadia away. 19 Many of the Jews had joined the women around Martha and Mary, to console them concerning their brother. 20 Then when Martha heard that Jesus was coming, she went and met him, but Mary stayed in the house. 21 Therefore Martha said to Jesus, "Lord, if you would have been here, my brother wouldn't have died. 22 Even now I know that whatever you ask of God, God will give you." 23 Jesus said to her, "Your brother will rise again."

24 Martha said to him, "I know that he will rise again in the resurrection at the last day."

25 Jesus said to her, "I am the resurrection and the life. He who believes in me will still live, even if he dies. 26 Whoever lives and believes in me will never die. Do you believe this?"

27 She said to him, "Yes, Lord. I have come to believe that you are the Christ, God's Son, he who comes into the world."

28 When she had said this, she went away and called Mary, her sister, secretly, saying, "The Teacher is here and is calling you."

29 When she heard this, she arose quickly and went to him. 30 Now Jesus had not yet come into the village, but was in the place where Martha met him. 31 Then the Jews who were with her in the house and were consoling her, when they saw Mary, that she rose up quickly and went out, followed her, saying, "She is going to the tomb to weep there." 32 Therefore when Mary came to where Jesus was and saw him, she fell down at his feet, saying to him, "Lord, if you would have been here, my brother wouldn't have died."

33 When Jesus therefore saw her weeping, and the Jews weeping who came with her, he groaned in the spirit, and was troubled, 34 and said, "Where have you laid him?"

They told him, "Lord, come and see."

35 Jesus wept.

36 The Jews therefore said, "See how much affection he had for him!" 37 Some of them said, "Couldn't this man, who opened the eyes of him who was blind, have also kept this man from dying?"

38 Jesus therefore, again groaning in himself, came to the tomb. Now it was a cave, and a stone lay against it. 39 Jesus said, "Take away the stone."

Martha, the sister of him who was dead, said to him, "Lord, by this time there is a stench, for he has been dead four days."

40 Jesus said to her, "Didn't I tell you that if you believed, you would see God's glory?"

41 So they took away the stone from the place where the dead man was lying. Jesus lifted up his eyes, and said, "Father, I thank you that you listened to me. 42 I know that you always listen to me, but because

of the multitude standing around I said this, that they may believe that you sent me." 43 When he had said this, he cried with a loud voice, "Lazarus, come out!"

44 He who was dead came out, bound hand and foot with wrappings, and his face was wrapped around with a cloth.

Jesus said to them, "Free him, and let him go."

45 Therefore many of the Jews who came to Mary and saw what Jesus did believed in him. 46 But some of them went away to the Pharisees and told them the things which Jesus had done. 47 The chief priests therefore and the Pharisees gathered a council, and said, "What are we doing? For this man does many signs. 48 If we leave him alone like this, everyone will believe in him, and the Romans will come and take away both our place and our nation."

49 But a certain one of them, Caiaphas, being high priest that year, said to them, "You know nothing at all, 50 nor do you consider that it is advantageous for us that one man should die for the people, and that the whole nation not perish." 51 Now he didn't say this of himself, but being high priest that year, he prophesied that Jesus would die for the nation, 52 and not for the nation only, but that he might also gather together into one the children of God who are scattered abroad. 53 So from that day forward they took counsel that they might put him to death. 54 Jesus therefore walked no more openly among the Jews, but departed from there into the country near the wilderness, to a city called Ephraim. He stayed there with his disciples.

55 Now the Passover of the Jews was at hand. Many went up from the country to Jerusalem before the Passover, to purify themselves. 56 Then they sought for Jesus and spoke one with another, as they stood in the temple, "What do you think—that he isn't coming to the feast at all?" 57 Now the chief priests and the Pharisees had commanded that if anyone knew where he was, he should report it, that they might seize him.

CHAPTER 14

Mary of Bethany

■ ■ ■

INTRODUCTION

Mary and Martha may well be called bookend sisters. That is, they are daughters of the same parents, but they look in opposite directions. Martha is the more active and even somewhat aggressive sister, while Mary is said to be the contemplative and quiet sort of woman.

Perhaps some prejudice has accrued to Mary (she is probably not Mary Magdalene) because she "sat at the feet" of Jesus; being taught directly by a spiritual leader would make her a disciple of that teacher, and this would be, according to some Christians, inappropriate for a woman.

And yet there is more that might explain prejudice against Mary and favoritism for her sister. Mary says very little in the biblical record. The only words recorded of her are those she repeats of her sister's complaint to Jesus: "Lord, if you had been here, my brother would not have died" (John 11:32). For the most part, she is silent, whether sitting at the feet of Jesus and learning from him, or pouring nard over his feet and wiping it with her hair (John !2:3). In fact, this last gesture has been seen by some scholars as her characteristic mode of communication, an action (in this case) of extravagant praise.

Susan Cain, in her admirable book *Quiet: The Power of Introverts in a World That Can't Stop Talking,* gives the following account of the rise of extroversion in America:

Self-help books have always loomed large in the American psyche. Many of the earliest conduct guides were religious parables, like *The Pilgrim's*

Progress, published in 1648, which warned readers to behave with restraint if they wanted to make it into heaven. The advice manuals of the nineteenth century were less religious but still preached the value of a noble character. They featured case studies of historical heroes like Abraham Lincoln, revered not only as a gifted communicator but also as a modest man who did not, as Ralph Waldo Emerson put it, "offend by superiority." They also celebrated regular people who lived highly moral lives. A popular 1899 manual called *Character: The Grandest Thing in the World,* featured a timid shop girl who gave away her meager earnings to a freezing beggar, then rushed off before anyone could see what she'd done. Her virtue, the reader understood, derived not only from her generosity but also from her wish to remain anonymous.

But by 1920, popular self-help guides had changed their focus from inner virtue to outer charm—"to know what to say and how to say it," as one manual put it. "To create a personality is power," advised another (page 22).

Now it may well be that learning to be a self-confident speaker, and creating a personality that means power for oneself, can be keys to worldly success, but we are not concerned with worldly success at the moment. We are concerned with spiritual matters, as was Bunyan's *Pilgrim's Progress.*

And so, assuming Susan Cain's insightful book to be correct, could this explain why those of us who find it difficult to divorce our lives from secular culture are likely to be unfair to introverts like Mary of Bethany, who says little but does a great deal?

For the benefit of those readers who find Mary's last three sentences puzzling, see John 4: 31-34 and Luke 24:41-43.

MARY OF BETHANY

MONOLOGUE

I *love* my sister and her practicality. If it weren't for her I'd forget to eat or set my things in order. But at times I don't *like* her very much.

She and I are opposites in some ways. She's my older sister, left to care for Lazarus and me. Our parents died you know. She's never forgotten to keep the house running no matter what. But I could not keep from thinking of what the Rabbi said the last time He was here. When Martha complained of my not helping, He said to her, "Mary has chosen what is better." I think He probably meant living for the Lord in heaven was more important than just living.

But nothing I can say to her will help her see his point. Surely not if He could not. She hears my voice as only the mewling of a dreamer or a child.

Sometimes I think of us as two halves of one complete person. Now what would that person be like? I suppose it would be most like the Rabbi. He would not eat when He'd seen Adonai work through him to save someone. Then, to prove that at his resurrection He was not a ghost, he ate. That's my goal in life.

MARY OF BETHANY

LUKE 10:

38 As they went on their way, he entered into a certain village, and a certain woman named Martha received him into her house. 39 She had a sister called Mary, who also sat at Jesus' feet, and heard his word. 40 But Martha was distracted with much serving, and she came up to him, and said, "Lord, don't you care that my sister left me to serve alone? Ask her therefore to help me."

41 Jesus answered her, "Martha, Martha, you are anxious and troubled about many things, 42 but one thing is needed. Mary has chosen the good part, which will not be taken away from her."

JOHN 11:

1 Now a certain man was sick, Lazarus from Bethany, of the village of Mary and her sister, Martha. 2 It was that Mary who had anointed the Lord with ointment and wiped his feet with her hair, whose brother, Lazarus, was sick.

3 The sisters therefore sent to him, saying, "Lord, behold, he for whom you have great affection is sick." 4 But when Jesus heard it, he said, "This sickness is not to death, but for the glory of God, that God's Son may be glorified by it." 5 Now Jesus loved Martha, and her sister, and Lazarus. 6 When therefore he heard that he was sick, he stayed two days in the place where he was. 7 Then after this he said to the disciples, "Let's go into Judea again." ...

17 So when Jesus came, he found that he had been in the tomb four days already. 18 Now Bethany was near Jerusalem, about fifteen stadia away. 19 Many of the Jews had joined the women around Martha and Mary, to console them concerning their brother. 20 Then when Martha heard that Jesus was coming, she went and met him, but Mary stayed in the house. 21 Therefore Martha said to Jesus, "Lord, if you would have been here, my brother wouldn't have died. 22 Even now I know that whatever you ask of God, God will give you." 23 Jesus said to her, "Your brother will rise again."

24 Martha said to him, "I know that he will rise again in the resurrection at the last day."

25 Jesus said to her, "I am the resurrection and the life. He who believes in me will still live, even if he dies. 26 Whoever lives and believes in me will never die. Do you believe this?"

27 She said to him, "Yes, Lord. I have come to believe that you are the Christ, God's Son, he who comes into the world."

28 When she had said this, she went away and called Mary, her sister, secretly, saying, "The Teacher is here and is calling you."

29 When she heard this, she arose quickly and went to him. 30 Now Jesus had not yet come into the village, but was in the place where Martha met him. 31 Then the Jews who were with her in the house and were consoling her, when they saw Mary, that she rose up quickly and went out, followed her, saying, "She is going to the tomb to weep there." 32 Therefore when Mary came to where Jesus was and saw him, she fell down at his feet, saying to him, "Lord, if you would have been here, my brother wouldn't have died."

33 When Jesus therefore saw her weeping, and the Jews weeping who came with her, he groaned in the spirit, and was troubled, 34 and said, "Where have you laid him?"

They told him, "Lord, come and see."

35 Jesus wept.

36 The Jews therefore said, "See how much affection he had for him!" 37 Some of them said, "Couldn't this man, who opened the eyes of him who was blind, have also kept this man from dying?"

38 Jesus therefore, again groaning in himself, came to the tomb. Now it was a cave, and a stone lay against it. 39 Jesus said, "Take away the stone."

Martha, the sister of him who was dead, said to him, "Lord, by this time there is a stench, for he has been dead four days."

40 Jesus said to her, "Didn't I tell you that if you believed, you would see God's glory?"

41 So they took away the stone from the place where the dead man was lying. Jesus lifted up his eyes, and said, "Father, I thank you that you listened to me. 42 I know that you always listen to me, but because of the multitude standing around I said this, that they may believe that you sent me." 43 When he had said this, he cried with a loud voice, "Lazarus, come out!"

44 He who was dead came out, bound hand and foot with wrappings, and his face was wrapped around with a cloth.

Jesus said to them, "Free him, and let him go."

12:

1 Then six days before the Passover, Jesus came to Bethany, where Lazarus was, who had been dead, whom he raised from the dead. 2 So they made him a supper there. Martha served, but Lazarus was one of those who sat at the table with him. 3 Therefore Mary took a pound* of ointment of pure nard, very precious, and anointed Jesus's feet and wiped his feet with her hair. The house was filled with the fragrance of the ointment. 4 Then Judas Iscariot, Simon's son, one of his disciples,

who would betray him, said, 5 "Why wasn't this ointment sold for three hundred denarii, and given to the poor?" 6 Now he said this, not because he cared for the poor, but because he was a thief, and having the money box, used to steal what was put into it. 7 But Jesus said, "Leave her alone. She has kept this for the day of my burial. 8 For you always have the poor with you, but you don't always have me."

CHAPTER 15

Moses

■ ■ ■

INTRODUCTION

As we read the Old Testament, we see that the people of ancient Israel are not always meek and submissive, either to their leaders or to the Lord. And perhaps their paramount rebellion in the Exodus occurs when they become impatient with Moses' prolonged absence from them while he is hearing God's words of the Law on Mt. Sinai.

They made for themselves a calf (actually the Hebrew word means young bull) of solid gold, worshiped it, sacrificed to it, and accepted it as their god, the god who freed them from slavery in Egypt (32:8). The identification of the "calf" as a young bull, together with the translation "indulge in revelry" in verse 6, meaning sexual play, points to their heresy as being worship of a fertility god instead of the true God.

This orgy, celebrating the fertility implicit in a young bull, is what Moses is faced with as he descends the mountain with God's tablets of the Ten Commandments. We are told by Bible scholars that the bull was a throwback to the Egyptian worship of Baal. And now, having laboriously brought these stubborn people out of Egypt according to God's command, Moses sees them backsliding.

If we judge Moses for his anger in this instance, we are by implication judging God as well, for He was prepared to destroy his chosen people for their apostasy, while it was Moses who apparently persuaded Him not to do so.

MOSES

MONOLOGUE

From water did I come, through water I have passed, and from the rock the water came to me. The Princess took me in as if I'd been a mewling puppy and her new pet. When I grew troublesome, I saw her not.

I killed a man was beating one of mine, then went to Midian. But tending flocks for

Jethro, I was called by "I Am Who I Am" toward an unconsuming flame. And with my sandals off, as if I were a slave, was told I must to Egypt, far from my flocks and simple serenity. All my objections and subterfuges He overcame.

The blood, the frogs, the locusts, darkness, death—each plague a hammer's fall on Pharaoh's land—released at last the pent community. We quit the ordered city, its commands that ruled each straw that went to bricks, and set upon a quest for promises.

We found the sea.

It stood before us as a liquid wall, and Pharaoh's armies closing to our rear. The people cried for Egypt's orderly and petty dominance, its tidy graves. But Adonai transformed the sea floor orderly for us, and turbid then for Pharaoh's men. We walked across as on the water's back. I never knew the east wind to blow such good.

But even so beneficent a pass as this had not remained in their memory. They cried for water, in despite of having cried for overmuch of it to pass. But the Lord stood with the promised rock while I tapped on it as it were a jar, and He cascaded them a living stream.

They were infirm of loyalty, forgot his loving-kindness. Again their fickle will was to return to Egypt, if not in personal return, then in their worship, celebration and their gratitude for liberties. I heard them singing, saw their naked dancing, and much more. And the Lord knew it all. His ire threw flames.

My face grew hot, I broke the tablets the Lord wrote, and I destroyed the bull. I have been angered in the past, but this was more. Much more.

MOSES

Exodus 31:

18 When he finished speaking with him on Mount Sinai, he gave Moses the two tablets of the covenant, stone tablets, written with God's finger.

Exodus 32:

1 When the people saw that Moses delayed coming down from the mountain, the people gathered themselves together to Aaron, and said to him, "Come, make us gods, which shall go before us; for as for this Moses, the man who brought us up out of the land of Egypt, we don't know what has become of him."

2 Aaron said to them, "Take off the golden rings, which are in the ears of your wives, of your sons, and of your daughters, and bring them to me."

3 All the people took off the golden rings which were in their ears, and brought them to Aaron. 4 He received what they handed him, fashioned it with an engraving tool, and made it a molded calf. Then they said, "These are your gods, Israel, which brought you up out of the land of Egypt."

5 When Aaron saw this, he built an altar before it; and Aaron made a proclamation, and said, "Tomorrow shall be a feast to God."

6 They rose up early on the next day, and offered burnt offerings, and brought peace offerings; and the people sat down to eat and to drink, and rose up to play.

7 God spoke to Moses, "Go, get down; for your people, who you brought up out of the land of Egypt, have corrupted themselves! 8 They have turned away quickly out of the way which I commanded them. They have made themselves a molded calf, and have worshiped it, and have sacrificed to it, and said, 'These are your gods, Israel, which brought you up out of the land of Egypt.' "

9 God said to Moses, "I have seen these people, and behold, they are a stiff-necked people. 10 Now therefore leave me alone, that my wrath

may burn hot against them, and that I may consume them; and I will make of you a great nation."

11 Moses begged God his God, and said, "God, why does your wrath burn hot against your people, that you have brought out of the land of Egypt with great power and with a mighty hand? 12 Why should the Egyptians speak, saying, 'He brought them out for evil, to kill them in the mountains, and to consume them from the surface of the earth?' Turn from your fierce wrath, and turn away from this evil against your people. 13 Remember Abraham, Isaac, and Israel, your servants, to whom you swore by your own self, and said to them, 'I will multiply your offspring as the stars of the sky, and all this land that I have spoken of I will give to your offspring, and they shall inherit it forever.' "

14 So God turned away from the evil which he said he would do to his people.

15 Moses turned, and went down from the mountain, with the two tablets of the covenant in his hand; tablets that were written on both their sides. They were written on one side and on the other. 16 The tablets were the work of God, and the writing was the writing of God, engraved on the tablets.

17 When Joshua heard the noise of the people as they shouted, he said to Moses, "There is the noise of war in the camp."

18 He said, "It isn't the voice of those who shout for victory. It is not the voice of those who cry for being overcome; but the noise of those who sing that I hear." 19 As soon as he came near to the camp, he saw the calf and the dancing. Then Moses' anger grew hot, and he threw the tablets out of his hands, and broke them beneath the mountain. 20 He took the calf which they had made, and burned it with fire, ground it to powder, and scattered it on the water, and made the children of Israel drink it.

21 Moses said to Aaron, "What did these people do to you, that you have brought a great sin on them?"

22 Aaron said, "Don't let the anger of my lord grow hot. You know the people, that they are set on evil. 23 For they said to me, 'Make us gods, which shall go before us. As for this Moses, the man who brought us up out of the land of Egypt, we don't know what has become of him.' 24 I said to them, 'Whoever has any gold, let them take it off.' So they gave it to me; and I threw it into the fire, and out came this calf."

25 When Moses saw that the people were out of control, (for Aaron had let them lose control, causing derision among their enemies), 26 then Moses stood in the gate of the camp, and said, "Whoever is on God's side, come to me!"

All the sons of Levi gathered themselves together to him. 27 He said to them, "The God of Israel, says, 'Every man put his sword on his thigh, and go back and forth from gate to gate throughout the camp, and every man kill his brother, and every man his companion, and every man his neighbor.' " 28 The sons of Levi did according to the word of Moses. About three thousand men fell of the people that day. 29 Moses said, "Consecrate yourselves today to God, for every man was against his son and against his brother, that he may give you a blessing today."

30 On the next day, Moses said to the people, "You have sinned a great sin. Now I will go up to God. Perhaps I shall make atonement for your sin."

31 Moses returned to God, and said, "Oh, this people have sinned a great sin, and have made themselves gods of gold. 32 Yet now, if you will, forgive their sin—and if not, please blot me out of your book which you have written."

33 God said to Moses, "Whoever has sinned against me, I will blot him out of my book. 34 Now go, lead the people to the place of which I have spoken to you. Behold, my angel shall go before you. Nevertheless, in the day when I punish, I will punish them for their sin." 35 God struck the people, because of what they did with the calf, which Aaron made.

NATHAN

CHAPTER 16

Nathan on David

■ ■ ■

INTRODUCTION

It is always interesting to think about the first human being to do certain things: kindle a controlled fire, invent the wheel, cook food, and so on. In reading the Bible, we often take for granted the literary form of the parable. Jesus uses it often and expects, at some point, that his disciples will understand the form. It's as though He assumes that they already know the form.

And indeed they should, if they've heard or read their own Bible of the time, the Hebrew Bible, our Old Testament. For it looks as if Nathan, in 2 Samuel, while he might not have invented the form, stumbled upon it almost in desperation and used it successfully with David while the King's guilt was still unrepented. Nathan does so, Scripture tells us, because the Lord "sent him to David" (11:27b).

But the Bible tells us nothing of how Nathan came up with the idea of using a fiction, one parallel to the reality (the definition of a parable), in order to awaken David's compassion for Uriah. How might that have developed in a man like Nathan?

NATHAN ON DAVID

MONOLOGUE

My way had been made easier if I'd stood mute beside the king who'd robbed his subject of his wife and then his life. But heaven spoke. No matter how I clapped my hands to ears, the charge persisted: "Bring him to repent!" But how? To open my lips in chastising him as if we were but man to common man would bring his glares, dismissals, and a standing on our different ranks. I like to think my own discomfort did not make me hesitant. But no good would it confer on him.

He is, you know, a man walled in by his accomplishments, be they on battlefield or bed. Those many foreskins cut from foreigners became Michal, an icon of his life in that he's callous to all loss in anyone but him. It's true he tried to keep the couple in their bed, but no, Uriah was more master of his lust than David in his luxury and ease.

And so I had a need to circumvent his close attention to himself. I thought my best approach to this would be a simple plea for just decision on an erring subject's crime. This woke a small compassion and he judged, then passed a proper sentence on himself, though not the one he would have pressed on lower-ranking men.

May Omnipotence declare that such self-criticism be implanted in our seed to sprout a thousand years from now. Let not our enemies be first to speak the diagnosis of our throbbing ills, but we ourselves, with care instead of hate, to lance our nation's boils precise—to heal, and not to leak a venom in the wound.

NATHAN ON DAVID

2 Samuel 12:

1 God sent Nathan to David. He came to him, and said to him, "There were two men in one city; the one rich, and the other poor. 2 The rich man had very many flocks and herds, 3 but the poor man had nothing, except one little ewe lamb, which he had bought and raised. It grew up together with him, and with his children. It ate of his own food, drank of his own cup, and lay in his bosom, and was like a daughter to him. 4 A traveler came to the rich man, and he spared to take of his own flock and of his own herd, to prepare for the wayfaring man who had come

to him, but took the poor man's lamb, and prepared it for the man who had come to him."

5 David's anger burned hot against the man, and he said to Nathan, "As God lives, the man who has done this deserves to die! 6 He must restore the lamb fourfold, because he did this thing, and because he had no pity!"

7 Nathan said to David, "You are the man. This is what God, the God of Israel, says: 'I anointed you king over Israel, and I delivered you out of the hand of Saul. 8 I gave you your master's house, and your master's wives into your bosom, and gave you the house of Israel and of Judah; and if that would have been too little, I would have added to you many more such things. 9 Why have you despised God's word, to do that which is evil in his sight? You have struck Uriah the Hittite with the sword, and have taken his wife to be your wife, and have slain him with the sword of the children of Ammon. 10 Now therefore the sword will never depart from your house, because you have despised me, and have taken Uriah the Hittite's wife to be your wife.'

11 "This is what God says: 'Behold, I will raise up evil against you out of your own house; and I will take your wives before your eyes, and give them to your neighbor, and he will lie with your wives in the sight of this sun. 12 For you did this secretly, but I will do this thing before all Israel, and before the sun.' "

13 David said to Nathan, "I have sinned against God."

Nathan said to David, "God also has put away your sin. You will not die. 14 However, because by this deed you have given great occasion to God's enemies to blaspheme, the child also who is born to you will surely die."

CHAPTER 17

Nicodemus

■ ■ ■

INTRODUCTION

A wife (let's call her Melissa) once went to her doctor because of nausea and excessive drowsiness. These are of course common symptoms of pregnancy, and Melissa mentioned this possibility in a passing remark. But the doctor, after looking at the woman's medical file, noticed similar symptoms about a year earlier, so interpreted this repetition as a psychosomatic disorder. But just as she was telling Melissa that it was "all in her head," a nurse entered the room with a lab report: the patient was pregnant. The doctor was furious with both the patient and the nurse for contradicting her diagnosis, in which she evidently took great pride.

This kind of professional pride, and the resulting offensive reaction, can take many forms, one of which may be the case of the early friction between Jesus and Nicodemus in this passage. Clearly Nicodemus is a respected member of the Sanhedrin and a teacher, not a man accustomed to being taught by others—certainly not accustomed to being lectured on seemingly impossible actions. But Nicodemus, despite his exemplary education in spiritual matters as a Pharisee, does not immediately see that when Jesus speaks of "being born again" he is not speaking of physical birth, but of a spiritual breakthrough in one's life.

This much is probably clear to most of us from the earlier passage in John's gospel. The only question is, How does this man come to be one of the two people (the other being Joseph of Arimathea) who seem to be disciples of Jesus in the later passage when they bury the Lord?

NICODEMUS

MONOLOGUE

How fickle all our faith can seem to be. True faith can sit so deep within our chest that we are blind to that close-hidden blazing light in us.

I was a Pharisee, a scribe, a member of the Sanhedrin, but unlike most I was discomfited by those who took the Law as rules one may evade by wit, as if they thought that Adonai, who made the Law, could be controlled by all their canniness.

It made no sense. A man can fully feed a crowd of thousands on a pair of fish and a few small loaves? A man can walk as well on water as on solid earth? A man can raise another, past three days dead, to life? No man can do such things unless the One on high had done them through that man. And if He has, then he who dares abuse that man will rot.

I said so, and they asked if I, like him, was Galilean and his partisan. I had been hungering for Adonai to show some signs of *hesed's* power that these oafs could not ignore, and now He had, but they had grown so cozy with their covenant that they assumed the Ruler of the universe was now irrelevant, so they of course resented any sign of His clear will, no matter how distinct.

I thought about our lone encounter when I walked though darkness into what I later saw was light. I uttered my belief that he was from the One, a plethora of witnesses, his acts. But he began to speak of being newly born as men—to me! One of the seventy who rule and teach the whole of Israel. I was enraged that I had stooped myself to one who only thought to pull a higher man down to his lowly stature. I took myself away to where the Ruler of the cosmos hid himself in seeming contradictions, in the murk between apostasy that I had scorned, and all those pure impossibilities displayed by one who'd seemed a hand of Adonai. I also took myself from studies, hence from rulership and its incessant quibbles on detail.

My indecision turned to solitude and nakedness of spirit to the Lord. There was no voice at all, not still or small or otherwise, except a weeping sound. I thought it was my wife, or else a child. It was my own. And then it turned torrential and I sobbed that I was so abandoned and discarded, buried, lost.

For days I took no food, no drink, and like King David, lay face down upon the ground and begged one word, one breath to comfort me. In all that darkness I began to see a man in jeweled robes, enthroned on gold, his legs not long enough to reach the floor. And then before him stood a ragged sort, his head so high it moved some stars aside.

This vision puzzled me until I saw the one enthroned more clearly, and his face was mine. The heaven-kissing man was that poor Galilean who had jostled so my bubble sense of self. So large in looks and in society I was, so midget-like in substance and in holy wisdom's grasp.

The unaccustomed shame astounded me, but when recovered partly I could see I was not left to rot but being taught by him who teaches well.

When he was dead, I went with Joseph, who'd obtained the corpse, and wrapped it in a modicum of herbs to satisfy what piece of Law was left in my still-arid soul. I thought by now there was a massive presence in the world, but I could hardly bear to look at it. And yet my soul was famished for the sense that it was real, and I'd conversed with it.

You know the rest. I cannot speak of it. This man was more than the anointed one, but my vocabulary cringes now.

NICODEMUS

John 3

1 Now there was a man of the Pharisees named Nicodemus, a ruler of the Jews. 2 The same came to him by night, and said to him, "Rabbi, we know that you are a teacher come from God, for no one can do these signs that you do, unless God is with him."

3 Jesus answered him, "Most certainly, I tell you, unless one is born anew, he can't see God's Kingdom."

4 Nicodemus said to him, "How can a man be born when he is old? Can he enter a second time into his mother's womb, and be born?"

5 Jesus answered, "Most certainly I tell you, unless one is born of water and spirit, he can't enter into God's Kingdom. 6 That which is born of the flesh is flesh. That which is born of the Spirit is spirit. 7 Don't marvel that I said to you, 'You must be born anew.' 8 The wind blows where it wants to, and you hear its sound, but don't know where it comes from and where it is going. So is everyone who is born of the Spirit."

9 Nicodemus answered him, "How can these things be?"

10 Jesus answered him, "Are you the teacher of Israel, and don't understand these things? 11 Most certainly I tell you, we speak that which we know, and testify of that which we have seen, and you don't receive our witness. 12 If I told you earthly things and you don't believe, how will you believe if I tell you heavenly things? 13 No one has ascended into heaven but he who descended out of heaven, the Son of Man, who is in heaven. 14 As Moses lifted up the serpent in the wilderness, even so must the Son of Man be lifted up, 15 that whoever believes in him should not perish, but have eternal life. 16 For God so loved the world, that he gave his one and only Son, that whoever believes in him should not perish, but have eternal life. 17 For God didn't send his Son into the world to judge the world, but that the world should be saved through him. 18 He who believes in him is not judged. He who doesn't believe has been judged already, because he has not believed in the name of the one and only Son of God. 19 This is the judgment, that the light has come into the world, and men loved the darkness rather than the light; for their works were evil. 20 For everyone who does evil hates the light, and doesn't come to the light, lest his works would be exposed. 21 But he who does the truth comes to the light, that his works may be revealed, that they have been done in God."

19:

39 Nicodemus, who at first came to Jesus by night, also came bringing a mixture of myrrh and aloes, about a hundred Roman pounds. 40 So they took Jesus' body, and bound it in linen cloths with the spices, as the custom of the Jews is to bury. 41 Now in the place where he was crucified there was a garden. In the garden was a new tomb in which no man had ever yet been laid. 42 Then because of the Jews' Preparation Day (for the tomb was near at hand) they laid Jesus there.

CHAPTER 18

Noah

■ ■ ■

INTRODUCTION

There exists both written (cuneiform) and geological evidence that supports in great part the Bible's account of a massive and catastrophic flood in the ancient Near East. Though the flood attested to by these sources was limited to the area near the Black Sea, the biblical version describes the deluge as world wide.

It is certain, however, that the ancient Jews saw the transformation of their world from an orderly dry-land society to an aquatic nightmare as nothing less than a return to the chaos that preceded the Creation. As such, the Flood required a renewal of the first Creation. And this second creation is to be accomplished by the ark and its inhabitants, both human and animal. They are, as it were, the seeds to sprout in the post-diluvian world.

And to continue the farming metaphor, God acts somewhat in the manner of a farmer whose first supply of sprouted seeds turned out to be mostly weeds. He picks from among them the most "upright" man He has created, Noah, and with him and his family and the rescued animals He sows again the world. And yet this renewed world soon separates itself from God again in a variety of ways.

NOAH

MONOLOGUE

The Lord spoke to me. He would end all flesh, for all the earth was filled with violence. Yet I must build an ark or ship of size prodigious for the chaos and calamity to come. The cause for this construction? To save a remnant of the world—my wife, myself, my sons and their three wives.

And with my family, a seed-stock of the animals. I did as I was told, then filled the ark. I saw before me such varieties of his creating as I'd never seen together, not before or since. Lions, sheep, wolves, goats, and so on to the satiety of space aboard. The braying, squealing, barking, roaring was cacophony that seemed, at certain moments, harmonized. The odors and the appetites conspired to overcome me with their amplitude and with the sweet, familiar stench of life.

These beasts, by contrast to the world we'd parted from, lived in plain honesty. And so should we, if I might have my way. No more the daily and deliberate splashing of the earth with blood of neighbors and acquaintances, or those one chanced upon. No more the thumb on scales, the telling of what had not come to pass, the good man's trust abused.

And yet that wood enclosure was my temporary tomb, my fictive death. My prayers in time flew out as if on wings to ask, Is this enough? Was this not our time to breathe, to see in sunlight once again and feel the wind, to walk on earth and see a tree break leaf? And finally, a sign: It is enough.

I have no notion why I was his choice, unless He put aside all my mistakes.

NOAH

GENESIS 7:

1 God said to Noah, "Come with all of your household into the ship, for I have seen your righteousness before me in this generation. 2 You shall take seven pairs of every clean animal with you, the male and his female. Of the animals that are not clean, take two, the male and his female. 3 Also of the birds of the sky, seven and seven, male and female, to keep seed alive on the surface of all the earth. 4 In seven days, I will cause it to rain on the earth for forty days and forty nights. I will destroy every living thing that I have made from the surface of the ground."

5 Noah did everything that God commanded him.

6 Noah was six hundred years old when the flood of waters came on the earth. 7 Noah went into the ship with his sons, his wife, and his sons' wives, because of the floodwaters. 8 Clean animals, unclean animals, birds, and everything that creeps on the ground 9 went by pairs to Noah into the ship, male and female, as God commanded Noah. 10 After the seven days, the floodwaters came on the earth. 11 In the six hundredth year of Noah's life, in the second month, on the seventeenth day of the month, on that day all the fountains of the great deep burst open, and the sky's windows opened. 12 It rained on the earth forty days and forty nights.

13 In the same day Noah, and Shem, Ham, and Japheth—the sons of Noah—and Noah's wife and the three wives of his sons with them, entered into the ship— 14 they, and every animal after its kind, all the livestock after their kind, every creeping thing that creeps on the earth after its kind, and every bird after its kind, every bird of every sort. 15 Pairs from all flesh with the breath of life in them went into the ship to Noah. 16 Those who went in, went in male and female of all flesh, as God commanded him; then God shut him in. 17 The flood was forty days on the earth. The waters increased, and lifted up the ship, and it was lifted up above the earth. 18 The waters rose, and increased greatly on the earth; and the ship floated on the surface of the waters. 19 The waters rose very high on the earth. All the high mountains that were under the whole sky were covered. 20 The waters rose fifteen cubits higher, and the mountains were covered. 21 All flesh died that moved on the earth, including birds, livestock, animals, every creeping thing that creeps on the earth, and every man. 22 All on the dry land, in whose nostrils was the breath of the spirit of life, died. 23 Every living thing was destroyed that was on the surface of the ground, including man, livestock, creeping things, and birds of the sky. They were destroyed from the earth. Only Noah was left, and those who were with him in the ship. 24 The waters flooded the earth one hundred fifty days.

9:

God said to Noah, "This is the token of the covenant which I have established between me and all flesh that is on the earth."

18 The sons of Noah who went out from the ship were Shem, Ham, and Japheth. Ham is the father of Canaan. 19 These three were the sons of Noah, and from these the whole earth was populated.

20 Noah began to be a farmer, and planted a vineyard. 21 He drank of the wine and got drunk. He was uncovered within his tent. 22 Ham, the father of Canaan, saw the nakedness of his father, and told his two brothers outside. 23 Shem and Japheth took a garment, and laid it on both their shoulders, went in backwards, and covered the nakedness of their father. Their faces were backwards, and they didn't see their father's nakedness. 24 Noah awoke from his wine, and knew what his youngest son had done to him. 25 He said,

"Canaan is cursed.

He will be a servant of servants to his brothers."

26 He said,

"Blessed be God, the God of Shem.

Let Canaan be his servant.

27 May God enlarge Japheth.

Let him dwell in the tents of Shem.

Let Canaan be his servant."

28 Noah lived three hundred fifty years after the flood. 29 All the days of Noah were nine hundred fifty years, and then he died.

CHAPTER 19

Paul (Saul)

■ ■ ■

INTRODUCTION

This is the passage which describes Saul's sudden and surprising conversion from persecutor of Christians to one of the new religion's most zealous supporters. Certainly the experience was brought upon him by a vision of the living Christ, a vision so intense, so much more than physical reality, that Saul not only was knocked to the ground by the force of it, but there from the ground held a brief conversation with the resurrected and ascended Jesus. And what is more, he later says he actually saw Jesus (1 Corinthians 9:1).

This experience is, in its own more shocking way, somewhat like Thomas's experience one week after Easter when he saw the risen and recognizable Jesus, saw the wounds and believed. Saul, in his epiphany of light, sees and hears Jesus and feels forced by his experience to reshape his entire life.

And that is because the "lord" he has heard speak and seen face-to-face has shamed him for persecuting Christians. I said above that Saul had to reshape his entire life, and that is true except for one part of his life, his formerly misplaced zeal. He had been extremely zealous about the eradication of this new Jewish sect; now, as Paul, he is extremely zealous about encouraging it, strengthening it, and correcting its errors. Do you suppose this was one of Christ's reason for recruiting Saul and making Paul? Can you think of any other reasons?

PAUL (SAUL)

MONOLOGUE

I knew that darkness closed the seeing eye, but never that excess of light could do so too, until that day upon the road when down the sun itself had come and entered in my head. It burst its light out through my eyes and threw me to the ground, blind to outward circumstance, but seeing still a being all of light.

It spoke to me, this power, so I called it *kyrie,* for at that moment I was called from what I was. It spoke, I'm sure it spoke. My name bypassed my ears and called me persecutor of himself, as royalty would do in speaking of his nation as himself. I won't reiterate our words; I'll only say the blow's own terror, the commanding voice, my physical prostration, all combined to shred me down to mere components.

I had now to make good sense of what made nothing like what men call common sense. I found the edifice of my religion was no building of dead stone or scroll of vellum, but held a life within, a spirit and a voice that made me fear for my own life and breath and sight. This was from heaven. I could but acquiesce.

I lived two lives, the one before the blast and that succeeding it. But that before was bent on cleansing threats to all I then believed. My present life weeds out some threats of innovative gospels, but oftener it's to encourage godly love within the body of the Lord. It was the unregarded part of my belief that slapped me off my horse so, like a seed, I could be cracked, the living water trickle in, and I could sprout and grow, not die and rot.

Instead of accolades for bringing bound believers in to see them stoned, I found myself extolling love, the kind that sees an Eden in our differences, the kind that makes one's love for hotheads just as warm as for judicious silence or the meek of heart.

PAUL (SAUL)

ACTS 9:

1 But Saul, still breathing threats and slaughter against the disciples of the Lord, went to the high priest 2 and asked for letters from him to the synagogues of Damascus, that if he found any who were of the Way, whether men or women, he might bring them bound to Jerusalem. 3 As he traveled, he got close to Damascus, and suddenly a light from the sky shone around him. 4 He fell on the earth, and heard a voice saying to him, "Saul, Saul, why do you persecute me?"

5 He said, "Who are you, Lord?"

The Lord said, "I am Jesus, whom you are persecuting. 6 But rise up and enter into the city, then you will be told what you must do."

7 The men who traveled with him stood speechless, hearing the sound, but seeing no one. 8 Saul arose from the ground, and when his eyes were opened, he saw no one. They led him by the hand, and brought him into Damascus. 9 He was without sight for three days, and neither ate nor drank.

PETER

CHAPTER 20

Peter

■ ■ ■

INTRODUCTION

C.S. Lewis once wrote of the Christian rite of communion, "The command, after all, was Take, eat: not Take, understand" (*Letters to Malcolm: Chiefly on Prayer*). His stated purpose in writing this was to put at peace the Christian division over the question of real presence by pointing out that *some* commands from the Lord are meant to evoke obedience, not analysis.

This is an issue that would not have occured to Peter. He was, as we would say, a "good-hearted man" who probably never had an analytic thought in his life. (He probably did not write the first letter ascribed to him, and he almost certainly did not write the second.) But he continued following Christ even when the crowd had fallen away, continued to try obeying, though he characteristically assumed he could do things he failed at when it came to the point of doing them. He acted before thinking, nearly drowning at one point as a result, and denying acquaintance with his Lord at another.

He knows certain things—that Jesus is the Messiah for instance—but he wouldn't have been able to tell you how he came to that conclusion. (Jesus had to tell him.) But then, not long after being spoken through by the Father, there speaks through him that all-too-human concern to try to save Jesus from his salvific death, a distraction that Jesus says is from Satan.

Peter is not perfect. (Which of us is?) But it is easy to love him.

PETER

MONOLOGUE

Yeah I did go back to fishing after they killed him. What else could I do? I let him down in every other way, why not this? Calling me Satan just for trying to save his life. How was I supposed to know his death was the key that would lock death away? In time, I mean. Good time.

There's always a complication, isn't there? You follow where they take him to trial, and keeping your head down does no good. So then you think, "Don't admit anything. You do and they'll stone you too." How did He know what I would say? And *when* I'd say it? The Man baffled me, always tacking and turning.

So they nailed him to a slab of wood, same wood He might've made something useful out of. You blame me for hiding? What would you of done? Climb up there on the cross with him? Sure you would. Never watched a crucifixion, have you? Never heard the screaming of men gone crazy, the begging from the ones who used to be so proud and dignified, never smelled what happens when the worst of pain tears a man inside-out and everything he ate and drank comes sliding down the tree. And you ask me why I didn't stay.

And the worst part was how He used my name, Cephas, Rock. I'm supposed to be the kind of man to steward his church. The kind of dummy, more like.

But then He walked and talked and ate and breathed again. What do you mean "How?" How should I know? All I know is He told me to feed his sheep. Three times. And three times He asked me if I loved him. Same number of times I'd said I didn't know him

Lots of things He did still amaze me. (All right, laugh. I know it doesn't take much.) What I wanted to say was the thing amazed me most was how He could forgive even me.

PETER

MATTHEW 14:

25 In the fourth watch of the night, Jesus came to them, walking on the sea. 26 When the disciples saw him walking on the sea, they were troubled, saying, "It's a ghost!" and they cried out for fear. 27 But immediately Jesus spoke to them, saying, "Cheer up! It is I! Don't be afraid."

28 Peter answered him and said, "Lord, if it is you, command me to come to you on the waters."

29 He said, "Come!"

Peter stepped down from the boat, and walked on the waters to come to Jesus. 30 But when he saw that the wind was strong, he was afraid, and beginning to sink, he cried out, saying, "Lord, save me!"

31 Immediately Jesus stretched out his hand, took hold of him, and said to him, "You of little faith, why did you doubt?"

MARK 8:

29 He said to them, "But who do you say that I am?"

Peter answered, "You are the Christ."

30 He commanded them that they should tell no one about him. 31 He began to teach them that the Son of Man must suffer many things, and be rejected by the elders, the chief priests, and the scribes, and be killed, and after three days rise again. 32 He spoke to them openly. Peter took him, and began to rebuke him. 33 But he, turning around, and seeing his disciples, rebuked Peter, and said, "Get behind me, Satan! For you have in mind not the things of God, but the things of men."

LUKE 22:

54 They seized him, and led him away, and brought him into the high priest's house. But Peter followed from a distance. 55 When they had kindled a fire in the middle of the courtyard, and had sat down together,

Peter sat among them. 56 A certain servant girl saw him as he sat in the light, and looking intently at him, said, "This man also was with him."

57 He denied Jesus, saying, "Woman, I don't know him."

58 After a little while someone else saw him, and said, "You also are one of them!"

But Peter answered, "Man, I am not!"

59 After about one hour passed, another confidently affirmed, saying, "Truly this man also was with him, for he is a Galilean!"

60 But Peter said, "Man, I don't know what you are talking about!" Immediately, while he was still speaking, a rooster crowed. 61 The Lord turned and looked at Peter. Then Peter remembered the Lord's word, how he said to him, "Before the rooster crows you will deny me three times." 62 He went out, and wept bitterly.

JOHN 21:

15 So when they had eaten their breakfast, Jesus said to Simon Peter, "Simon, son of Jonah, do you love me more than these?"

He said to him, "Yes, Lord; you know that I have affection for you."

He said to him, "Feed my lambs." 16 He said to him again a second time, "Simon, son of Jonah, do you love me?"

He said to him, "Yes, Lord; you know that I have affection for you."

He said to him, "Tend my sheep." 17 He said to him the third time, "Simon, son of Jonah, do you have affection for me?"

Peter was grieved because he asked him the third time, "Do you have affection for me?" He said to him, "Lord, you know everything. You know that I have affection for you."

Jesus said to him, "Feed my sheep.

RAHAB

CHAPTER 21

Rahab

■ ■ ■

INTRODUCTION

Rahab was a woman whose reputation is difficult to settle. She was a prostitute living in Jericho who committed treason against her own city-kingdom. Yet she is listed an ancestress of Jesus in Matthew 1:5, and is highly praised in Hebrews 11:31 (for her faith) and in James 2:25 (for her good works).

The two Israelite spies Joshua sends into Jericho lodge with her, probably because her reputation as a prostitute would make their presence less conspicuous. But her address to the spies in 2:9-14 is a mixture of awe at the Israelites' and their God's military successes, together with a genius for survival. She fears for her own life and for that of her family if and when the Jews attack Jericho.

As an example of her tactical ingenuity, she sends the spies off in a direction *away* from Joshua's encampment so that they may hide in the caves of the hills where the King of Jericho's men will not search for them. Then, when three days have passed with no sign of the hidden spies, the king's men return empty-handed, and the spies safely report back to Joshua. One thing about Rahab is a certainty: she is an extremely clever survivor.

RAHAB

MONOLOGUE

There came two sons of Israel and knocked in stealth, at night. It was the common way. A decent man will rarely seek my door. So I was ready, told them to slide their silver below the door before I opened it. I keep a dagger in my gown. I am not named a dragon as an empty jest. When I had pocketed their mites, I slipped the latch and let them enter in my house. But they would none of it. To what they'd paid, they added further coins, requesting but a bowl of stew meat and a night of sleep. I fed them and I put them on the roof to sleep.

At dawn they were afoot and asking me about the city: what the force of men, what water and provisions lay in store. I had me here a brace of Jewish spies. And I was not the only one to know. The King had spies as well, who spied upon the spies. He sent some soldiers and demanded these, explaining carefully that these were not my kind of customer but (ha!) were spies.

They thought me stupid so I gave them more stupidity: Ah yes, there had been men, and they had paid me well, but told me none of where they came from or by whom were sent. And when the signal sounded that the city gate would shut, they'd gone as they had come, in darkness. Chase them, I said, then called them cowards if they cringed within the walls. So off they ran, afraid my public tongue would shame their swords.

When they were quit, I climbed up to the roof where I had hidden them among the flax, and told them what I understood of them. They were the merest but the sharpest tip of Israel's strong spear. But greater than their manly arms, there was an unseen force that piled up seas to either side for them. The Amorites and others had collapsed like slaves who fall to kneel before their lord.

I said the men of Jericho were quaking now that Hebrews and their adamantine God had aimed their eyes at us. Their God was strong, ours only customary love of home, their names just facile words for what we like.

I made them swear to safety for my house, that is, my family's and mine. They swore with some provisos, all acceptable. The crimson cord that hung like dripping blood upon my window frame became my sign. It saved me and my line as sure as if their future kings depended there.

RAHAB

JOSHUA 2

1 Joshua the son of Nun secretly sent two men out of Shittim as spies, saying, "Go, view the land, including Jericho." They went and came into the house of a prostitute whose name was Rahab, and slept there.

2 The king of Jericho was told, "Behold, men of the children of Israel came in here tonight to spy out the land."

3 Jericho's king sent to Rahab, saying, "Bring out the men who have come to you, who have entered into your house; for they have come to spy out all the land."

4 The woman took the two men and hid them. Then she said, "Yes, the men came to me, but I didn't know where they came from. 5 About the time of the shutting of the gate, when it was dark, the men went out. Where the men went, I don't know. Pursue them quickly. You may catch up with them." 6 But she had brought them up to the roof, and hidden them under the stalks of flax which she had laid in order on the roof. 7 The men pursued them along the way to the fords of the Jordan River. As soon as those who pursued them had gone out, they shut the gate. 8 Before they had lain down, she came up to them on the roof. 9 She said to the men, "I know that God has given you the land, and that the fear of you has fallen upon us, and that all the inhabitants of the land melt away before you. 10 For we have heard how God dried up the water of the Red Sea before you, when you came out of Egypt; and what you did to the two kings of the Amorites, who were beyond the Jordan, to Sihon and to Og, whom you utterly destroyed. 11 As soon as we had heard it, our hearts melted, and there wasn't any more spirit in any man, because of you: for God, he is God in heaven above, and on earth beneath. 12 Now therefore, please swear to me by God, since I have dealt kindly with you, that you also will deal kindly with my father's house, and give me a true sign; 13 and that you will save alive my father, my mother, my brothers, and my sisters, and all that they have, and will deliver our lives from death."

14 The men said to her, "Our life for yours, if you don't talk about this business of ours; and it shall be, when God gives us the land, that we will deal kindly and truly with you."

15 Then she let them down by a cord through the window; for her house was on the side of the wall, and she lived on the wall. 16 She said to them, "Go to the mountain, lest the pursuers find you. Hide yourselves there three days, until the pursuers have returned. Afterward, you may go your way."

17 The men said to her, "We will be guiltless of this your oath which you've made us to swear. 18 Behold, when we come into the land, tie this line of scarlet thread in the window which you used to let us down. Gather to yourself into the house your father, your mother, your brothers, and all your father's household. 19 It shall be that whoever goes out of the doors of your house into the street, his blood will be on his head, and we will be guiltless. Whoever is with you in the house, his blood shall be on our head, if any hand is on him. 20 But if you talk about this business of ours, then we shall be guiltless of your oath which you've made us to swear."

21 She said, "Let it be as you have said." She sent them away, and they departed. Then she tied the scarlet line in the window.

22 They went, and came to the mountain, and stayed there three days, until the pursuers had returned. The pursuers sought them all along the way, but didn't find them.

6:

22 Joshua said to the two men who had spied out the land, "Go into the prostitute's house, and bring the woman and all that she has out from there, as you swore to her." 23 The young men who were spies went in, and brought out Rahab with her father, her mother, her brothers, and all that she had. They also brought out all of her relatives, and they set them outside of the camp of Israel. 24 They burned the city with fire, and all that was in it. Only they put the silver, the gold, and the vessels of bronze and of iron into the treasury of God's

house. 25 But Rahab the prostitute, her father's household, and all that she had, Joshua saved alive. She lives in the middle of Israel to this day, because she hid the messengers, whom Joshua sent to spy out Jericho.

CHAPTER 22

The Rich Young Ruler

■ ■ ■

INTRODUCTION

We have all read of this encounter; but perhaps we neglect to ask ourselves why the rich young man approaches Jesus with his question at all if he is so satisfied with his life as it is. After all, he not only has his youth, he also has much wealth. He's not crippled, blind or lame. What does he want? Well, according to the question he asks Jesus, he wants eternal life.

On questioning him, Jesus hears that the young man has never committed adultery or murder, stolen, given false witness or defrauded anyone, and he has honored his parents. And that's when Mark tells us that Jesus felt affection for the man's obedience *thus far.* But one further question from Jesus finds that the man has an idol that is compromising his love for God—his wealth, his possessions.

Now why has Jesus left this out of his list from the Ten Commandments? Could it be that Jesus knows of the man's sin, but nevertheless hopes to cure him of it? And if that is so, then we are back to our earlier question. Why does this partially admirable young man ask Jesus' approval of his life? Could it be that he's hoping Jesus will either neglect or forgive the man's violation of the other four commandments and promise him "eternal life" anyway?

THE RICH YOUNG RULER

MONOLOGUE

People prattle. That, I'm sure, is how He knew of my extended family of relatives, slaves, houses, oxen, sheep, goats, asses and cache of silver. "Give all to the poor," He said to me, and I, bedraggled in my birth, who scratched from sullen soil a kind of ease, should throw it all away. That would be to lose my sweat-stained gains to layabouts and curs.

I used great courtesy in greeting, which He plucked away in leaving of my lips. "Why do you call me good?" Good seemed to me a thing an itinerant rabbi might have relished, though a trait of Elohim. But for this candy to such a one in need, I'm paid a tart reply. It was, in fact, far from the sop I'd hoped for from this homeless holy man—some recognition of my righteousness.

Instead, my Eden here today, my solid good, he demanded from me, with the only payment offered, at least the only one in sight, was following his leadership. I stood considering how to refuse without inviting blame from lookers-on, but decided to keep my silence. Still, when I was yet in hearing, he made me look grotesque, a gross and monstrous camel who aspired to slip like slender thread beyond the needle's eye.

I ask you, if adherence to the Law is paid in sweet prosperity, who is this teacher to say no?

THE RICH YOUNG RULER

MATTHEW 19:

16 Behold, one came to him and said, "Good teacher, what good thing shall I do, that I may have eternal life?"

17 He said to him, "Why do you call me good? No one is good but one, that is, God. But if you want to enter into life, keep the commandments."

18 He said to him, "Which ones?"

Jesus said, " 'You shall not murder.' 'You shall not commit adultery.' 'You shall not steal.' 'You shall not offer false testimony.' 19 'Honor your father and your mother.' And, 'You shall love your neighbor as yourself.' "

20 The young man said to him, "All these things I have observed from my youth. What do I still lack?"

21 Jesus said to him, "If you want to be perfect, go, sell what you have, and give to the poor, and you will have treasure in heaven; and come, follow me." 22 But when the young man heard the saying, he went away sad, for he was one who had great possessions. 23 Jesus said to his disciples, "Most certainly I say to you, a rich man will enter into the Kingdom of Heaven with difficulty. 24 Again I tell you, it is easier for a camel to go through a needle's eye, than for a rich man to enter into God's Kingdom."

25 When the disciples heard it, they were exceedingly astonished, saying, "Who then can be saved?"

26 Looking at them, Jesus said, "With men this is impossible, but with God all things are possible."

27 Then Peter answered, "Behold, we have left everything, and followed you. What then will we have?"

28 Jesus said to them, "Most certainly I tell you that you who have followed me, in the regeneration when the Son of Man will sit on the throne of his glory, you also will sit on twelve thrones, judging the twelve tribes of Israel. 29 Everyone who has left houses, or brothers, or sisters, or father, or mother, or wife, or children, or lands, for my name's sake, will receive one hundred times, and will inherit eternal life. 30 But many will be last who are first; and first who are last.

CHAPTER 23

Ruth

■ ■ ■

INTRODUCTION

The story of Ruth, Naomi and Boaz contains four moments at which a choice is made. And all four of these choices, as they are made, lead to Ruth, a Moabite by birth, becoming an ancestress of Jesus.

The four points in the narrative are these:

1. On the Moabite highway, where Naomi and Ruth discuss their futures, their final decision being for the daughter-in-law to follow her mother-in-law.
2. The harvest scene, with Boaz approving of Ruth's gleaning from his field.
3. On the threshing floor, when Ruth and Boaz sleep together.
4. At the city gate, where a solemn civil hearing allows for the marriage of Boaz and Ruth.

Taken together, these four turning points appear to have been Providentially decided.

The only one of these points that might be somewhat controversial is number three. But the Bible scholar Edward F. Campbell, Jr. makes short work of our prudery as to the possibility of intercourse in this instance. He points out many word choices in the original Hebrew which lead in this direction, the most explicit of which is the word for "feet" in 3:4 and again in 3:14. Campbell interprets this as "a standard

[Hebrew] euphemism for the sexual organs" (*The Anchor Bible,* vol. 7, page 131).

As for the question of their marriage, the story clearly combines laws from both Deuteronomy 25:5-10 and a pair of passages from Leviticus, 25:25 and 27:9-33.

RUTH

MONOLOGUE

My mother's house behind me, I married well a son of sweet Naomi, she who was hard oppressed by losing her Elimelech. She then was further desolate by loss of sons, first my Mahlon, then Orpah's Kilion. We neither of us were yet given motherhood to offer her a progeny. By then, the famine in her native land relieved, she made to quit our Moab and return.

We three set out. Naomi stopped and thought, then urged retreat on both our parts to Moab, to our first mothers we had left behind. With Orpah it was well. She loved the ways of Moab. But Naomi's kindness was an April in my life. Through all her pain brought down by her Shaddai, she never once relaxed her reverence for him, and went back home to Bethlehem to catch a drop of his new rain upon her tongue. Such trust I had not known. I would resemble her.

In Bethlehem, the harvest had begun. The barley fields were profligate with grain, and we without a seed to carry on. "But then," I said to her, "at least I might go gleaning in the footsteps of some man whose harvesting has made him merciful." She said to go, and in the field some force led me to glean my seed in furrows that one Boaz held as his. And he observed, enquired some men of me, and then to me: "Be you content to gather on my land. Remain among my maids and keep you safe. The boisterous young men I have adjured to leave you to yourself inviolate." He spoke in ancient words, but I was glad to have them in my ears. He said the help I gave Naomi in her woe was notable.

That night, repairing to Naomi's hut, I'm asked whose generosity was this that I should bring so great a sack of grain. I said the name of Boaz, which she blessed, and seemed to think her God began to smile. She said this Boaz was close in kinship and to stay within protective fellowship of maids. My mother had approved, and so I did.

When all the grain was in, it yet remained to palpitate it on the threshing floor. Naomi said the time had come to seek a home for me when she should breathe her last. She said to wash, anoint myself, put on my comeliest of robes, and go to where the men were threshing and the seed was bared. She said when Boaz laid him down to sleep, to mark the place for when the lights were all put out, and then to lift the cover from his leg and lie with him—that I should do his will.

The day that followed he arranged to buy my life and free me from sterility. We wed, and from us came a son, Obed, Naomi's son as well. And from this son came Jesse who produced Davidic sons.

His greatest kindness of them all, it seems, is that the God of Israel accepts among his sheep a Moabitic ewe, a foreign widow, desperate for food, and makes her mother to the finest king.

RUTH

RUTH 1:

They went on the way to return to the land of Judah. 8 Naomi said to her two daughters-in-law, "Go, return each of you to her mother's house. May God deal kindly with you, as you have dealt with the dead, and with me. 9 May God grant you that you may find rest, each of you in the house of her husband."

Then she kissed them, and they lifted up their voices, and wept. 10 They said to her, "No, but we will return with you to your people."

11 Naomi said, "Go back, my daughters. Why do you want to go with me? Do I still have sons in my womb, that they may be your husbands? 12 Go back, my daughters, go your way; for I am too old to have

a husband. If I should say, 'I have hope,' if I should even have a husband tonight, and should also bear sons; 13 would you then wait until they were grown? Would you then refrain from having husbands? No, my daughters, for it grieves me seriously for your sakes, for God's hand has gone out against me."

14 They lifted up their voices, and wept again; then Orpah kissed her mother-in-law, but Ruth joined with her. 15 She said, "Behold, your sister-in-law has gone back to her people, and to her god. Follow your sister-in-law."

16 Ruth said, "Don't urge me to leave you, and to return from following you, for where you go, I will go; and where you stay, I will stay. Your people will be my people, and your God my God. 17 Where you die, I will die, and there I will be buried. May God do so to me, and more also, if anything but death parts you and me."

18 When she saw that she was determined to go with her, she stopped urging her.

19 So they both went until they came to Bethlehem.

2:

8 Then Boaz said to Ruth, "Listen, my daughter. Don't go to glean in another field, and don't go from here, but stay here close to my maidens. 9 Let your eyes be on the field that they reap, and go after them. Haven't I commanded the young men not to touch you? When you are thirsty, go to the vessels, and drink from that which the young men have drawn."

10 Then she fell on her face, and bowed herself to the ground, and said to him, "Why have I found favor in your sight, that you should take knowledge of me, since I am a foreigner?"

11 Boaz answered her, "I have been told all about what you have done for your mother-in-law since the death of your husband, and how you have left your father and your mother, and the land of your birth, and have come to a people that you didn't know before. 12 May God

repay your work, and a full reward be given to you from God, the God of Israel, under whose wings you have come to take refuge."

3:

1 Naomi her mother-in-law said to her, "My daughter, shall I not seek rest for you, that it may be well with you? 2 Now isn't Boaz our kinsman, with whose maidens you were? Behold, he will be winnowing barley tonight on the threshing floor. 3 Therefore wash yourself, anoint yourself, get dressed, and go down to the threshing floor, but don't make yourself known to the man until he has finished eating and drinking. 4 It shall be, when he lies down, that you shall note the place where he is lying. Then you shall go in, uncover his feet, and lay down. Then he will tell you what to do."

5 She said to her, "All that you say, I will do." 6 She went down to the threshing floor, and did everything that her mother-in-law told her. 7 When Boaz had eaten and drunk, and his heart was merry, he went to lie down at the end of the heap of grain. She came softly, uncovered his feet, and laid down. 8 At midnight, the man was startled and turned himself; and behold, a woman lay at his feet. 9 He said, "Who are you?"

She answered, "I am Ruth your servant. Therefore spread the corner of your garment over your servant; for you are a near kinsman."

10 He said, "You are blessed by God, my daughter. You have shown more kindness in the latter end than at the beginning, because you didn't follow young men, whether poor or rich. 11 Now, my daughter, don't be afraid. I will do to you all that you say; for all the city of my people knows that you are a worthy woman. 12 Now it is true that I am a near kinsman. However, there is a kinsman nearer than I. 13 Stay this night, and in the morning, if he will perform for you the part of a kinsman, good. Let him do the kinsman's duty. But if he will not do the duty of a kinsman for you, then I will do the duty of a kinsman for you, as God lives. Lie down until the morning."

4:

5 Then Boaz said, "On the day you buy the field from the hand of Naomi, you must buy it also from Ruth the Moabitess, the wife of the dead, to raise up the name of the dead on his inheritance."

6 The near kinsman said, "I can't redeem it for myself, lest I endanger my own inheritance. Take my right of redemption for yourself; for I can't redeem it."

7 Now this was the custom in former time in Israel concerning redeeming and concerning exchanging, to confirm all things: a man took off his shoe, and gave it to his neighbor; and this was the way of formalizing transactions in Israel. 8 So the near kinsman said to Boaz, "Buy it for yourself," then he took off his shoe.

9 Boaz said to the elders, and to all the people, "You are witnesses today, that I have bought all that was Elimelech's, and all that was Chilion's and Mahlon's, from the hand of Naomi. 10 Moreover Ruth the Moabitess, the wife of Mahlon, I have purchased to be my wife, to raise up the name of the dead on his inheritance, that the name of the dead may not be cut off from among his brothers, and from the gate of his place. You are witnesses today."

11 All the people who were in the gate, and the elders, said, "We are witnesses. May God make the woman who has come into your house like Rachel and like Leah, which both built the house of Israel; and treat you worthily in Ephrathah, and be famous in Bethlehem. 12 Let your house be like the house of Perez, whom Tamar bore to Judah, of the offspring which God will give you by this young woman."

13 So Boaz took Ruth, and she became his wife; and he went in to her, and God enabled her to conceive, and she bore a son.

CHAPTER 24

Samson

■ ■ ■

INTRODUCTION

Once again we have before us a proud man somewhat like Nicodemus; like him in being proud, but unlike Nicodemus in being proud of his physical strength and cleverness instead of his knowledge. Samson is like the stereotype of the weightlifter who feels that his great strength gives him the right to indulge his lusts with any woman just because "she looks good to [him]" (Judges 14:3 New American Standard Version). This is the first step he takes toward his own ruin, and not only with the woman of Timnah, but again later with Delilah. (It's true that we are told this is part of God's plan "to confront the Philistines," but Samson is the man God outfitted with these particular traits, which lead and enable him to destroy the Philistines.)

Clearly this hero is depicted as a man of incredible endurance and strength. After his visit to a prostitute in Gaza, at midnight he went out and "took hold of the doors of the city gate, together with the two posts, and tore them loose, bar and all" (16:3). Then he carried all of this heavy material 38 miles away, and mostly uphill, to Hebron. The four chapters in Judges that tell his story are possibly best read as the story of a Jewish superhero who realizes his life's mission only after he has lost his strength, his dignity, and his political leadership. It is then that his immense strength is restored.

SAMSON

MONOLOGUE

Not by my choice am I a Nazirite. To set apart one's life—no wine to drink, with head of uncut ropy hair, to have to go around whatever corpse I come across, all as if I were a timid and bedraggled maiden—this was no thing befitting a man like me.

I'd tasted nothing certain of my strength until I went to Timnah. Both my hands were weaponless. A lion leaped at me. I gripped its nape and bashed it on a rock to death. And then, to test me more, I tore apart its sinews and its bones. The jackals and the heat would strip it dry. And then, with luck, the bees would find a home. Then I'd find honey to take to my own home. It happened so, and I saw the sign: By my own might, the lion of oppression would be torn. From it would come a sweetness in the mouth of Israel.

I made of it a riddle for the Greeks. Their dull thoughts could never ravel it out. But woman's tears and Greek deceit betrayed the game. I went home irate.

It was the same but larger when I took another Greek as wife. Delilah sold my life to them for certain silver coins. I told you that my hair was under vow to be unrazed. I'd broken something of a vow before, the honey from the lion's skull. But that, I think, was signed by Elohim in placing honey there. This time I had put my woman in the place of God. (Adam's fault, I'm sure.) She mowed my strength from off my head.

The Greeks put me in chains I had no might to break. It left me, as had the Lord. They harvested my eyes like picking grapes. It overjoyed them more than jugs of wine. And so I must needs turn the grindstone for them, as if I were a lowly ass or ox. And every grain of wheat I prayed to be an eye of Philistines.

In time my hair grew out again. Not all there had been, but it sufficed the Lord. He seeks occasion to set right our faults. My power grew. They put me on display. I prayed again. This time that, for each eye of mine they plucked, there be a pillar close at hand. And let the two of them support the crowd-packed building. I was led to them. And when

I pushed them down, the little lords within and on the roof all companied with me in death.

This was a better bargain than before. In place of silver coins to buy a foolish Jew, I spent one Jew to buy three-thousand Greeks. And freedom on its way to Israel.

SAMSON

JUDGES 13:

3 God's angel appeared to the woman, and said to her, "See now, you are barren and childless; but you shall conceive, and bear a son. 4 Now therefore please beware and drink no wine nor strong drink, and don't eat any unclean thing: 5 for, behold, you shall conceive, and give birth to a son. No razor shall come on his head; for the child shall be a Nazirite to God from the womb. He shall begin to save Israel out of the hand of the Philistines."

14:

1 Samson went down to Timnah, and saw a woman in Timnah of the daughters of the Philistines. 2 He came up, and told his father and his mother, and said, "I have seen a woman in Timnah of the daughters of the Philistines. Now therefore get her for me as my wife."

3 Then his father and his mother said to him, "Isn't there a woman among your brothers' daughters, or among all my people, that you go to take a wife of the uncircumcised Philistines?"

Samson said to his father, "Get her for me, for she pleases me well."

4 But his father and his mother didn't know that it was of God; for he sought an occasion against the Philistines. Now at that time the Philistines ruled over Israel.

16:

1 Samson went to Gaza, and saw there a prostitute, and went in to her. 2 The Gazites were told, "Samson is here!" They surrounded him, and laid wait for him all night in the gate of the city, and were quiet all

the night, saying, "Wait until morning light, then we will kill him." 3 Samson lay until midnight, and arose at midnight, and laid hold of the doors of the gate of the city, and the two posts, and plucked them up, bar and all, and put them on his shoulders, and carried them up to the top of the mountain that is before Hebron.

4 It came to pass afterward, that he loved a woman in the valley of Sorek, whose name was Delilah. 5 The lords of the Philistines came up to her, and said to her, "Entice him, and see in which his great strength lies, and by what means we may prevail against him, that we may bind him to afflict him; and we will each give you eleven hundred pieces of silver."

6 Delilah said to Samson, "Please tell me where your great strength lies, and what you might be bound to afflict you." ...

19 She made him sleep on her knees; and she called for a man, and shaved off the seven locks of his head; and she began to afflict him, and his strength went from him. 20 She said, "The Philistines are upon you, Samson!"

He awoke out of his sleep, and said, "I will go out as at other times, and shake myself free." But he didn't know that God had departed from him. 21 The Philistines laid hold on him, and put out his eyes; and they brought him down to Gaza, and bound him with fetters of bronze; and he ground at the mill in the prison. 22 However the hair of his head began to grow again after he was shaved.

23 The lords of the Philistines gathered them together to offer a great sacrifice to Dagon their god, and to rejoice; for they said, "Our god has delivered Samson our enemy into our hand." 24 When the people saw him, they praised their god; for they said, "Our god has delivered our enemy and the destroyer of our country, who has slain many of us, into our hand."

25 When their hearts were merry, they said, "Call for Samson, that he may entertain us." They called for Samson out of the prison; and he performed before them. They set him between the pillars; 26 and

Samson said to the boy who held him by the hand, "Allow me to feel the pillars whereupon the house rests, that I may lean on them."

27 Now the house was full of men and women; and all the lords of the Philistines were there; and there were on the roof about three thousand men and women, who saw while Samson performed. 28 Samson called to God, and said, "Lord God, remember me, please, and strengthen me, please, only this once, God, that I may be at once avenged of the Philistines for my two eyes." 29 Samson took hold of the two middle pillars on which the house rested, and leaned on them, the one with his right hand, and the other with his left. 30 Samson said, "Let me die with the Philistines!" He bowed himself with all his might; and the house fell on the lords, and on all the people who were therein.

CHAPTER 25

Satan

■ ■ ■

INTRODUCTION

Satan, in the book of Job and other early books of the Bible, is referred to by the title of his office, "the satan," which means accuser and at that stage is not his personal name. This has caused some scholars to see this early figure of the satan as acting with something approaching an amorality appropriate to his duty, not evil.

But there are signs even in the early stages of the satan's known career that his motives are not even-handed. In Job 1:10-11 and 2:5, he addresses God as "you," not as "my lord" as even mortal kings were addressed. This indicates the satan's attitude as being God's equal, an act of effrontery resulting from sinful pride.

And this effrontery is given further expression when the satan speaks to God as if he were commanding the Lord in 1:11 when he says, "But stretch out your hand and strike everything he has," and in 2:5 when he says, "But stretch out your hand and strike his flesh and bones." This is followed immediately by, "and he will surely curse you to your face," something Job steadfastly refuses to do, but which allows us to see clearly that the satan is far from prepared to test Job's faith justly. In fact, it implies that God's repeated statements of high esteem for Job are either a lie or an error, something unthinkable to anyone who recognizes some of the immense gulf between God's high holiness and the imperfection of his creatures, the satan included of course.

No matter whether "the satan" or "Satan," he is more like the attorney for the prosecution in our culture, one who has no attorney for the defense to balance his attacks on the defendant. Instead there is God, who sets limits on the harm he can inflict on Job. This allows God to demonstrate how far the satan will go in indulging his destructive tendencies.

And then this is the tempter, Satan with a capital S, who tests Jesus in Matthew 4:1-11 and fails again, even more miserably than with Job. Also, this is the Satan in John 13:27 who ends all hope for Judas's soul by entering into him. This is the same Satan whom Jesus tells the apostles He saw falling after they return from their mission, reporting their successes in healing and casting out demons. If the wholesome successes of these ordinary people were the final cause of God's casting Satan down to hell, then perhaps we can assume that Satan has been irretrievably proven to have been on the wrong side all along (Luke 10:18).

SATAN

MONOLOGUE

High Chief of all the Seraphim is what I am. For still and ever I deserve that title and that rare estate. Believe that I, from that exalted rank beyond all angelic beings, paid the stipulated obeisance to the maker, he whose creations are told they must obey, kneel before him, pull the forelock, take off their shoes, and so abase themselves. Who will expect such fawning from such majesty as I possess? Add to that thus more: by what false logic does the builder demand subservience from the house he builds?

I saw it therefore as correct, as well as proper to my high position, that I counsel him against devising creatures of free will and thought like ours, then thrust it in a decadent receptacle of flesh. What would it profit him? More to the point, would it not inconvenience those of us pure spirits, magnificent as we turned out to be?

But no, he must needs have his sentimental way. And even when the first two hybrid animals devised a way to disobey, he would persist throughout their filthy generations. He caught me once with Job, but I too can persist, and did until his pet was nearly dead.

At last, he fell into a girl, himself disguised. I recognized him only as his son and put him through his paces. He's thrown me to the ground a set of times, but I'll not call him master till no pride remains in me.

SATAN

Job 1:

6 Now on the day when God's sons came to present themselves before God, Satan also came among them. 7 God said to Satan, "Where have you come from?"

Then Satan answered God, and said, "From going back and forth in the earth, and from walking up and down in it."

8 God said to Satan, "Have you considered my servant, Job? For there is no one like him in the earth, a blameless and an upright man, one who fears God, and turns away from evil."

9 Then Satan answered God, and said, "Does Job fear God for nothing? 10 Haven't you made a hedge around him, and around his house, and around all that he has, on every side? You have blessed the work of his hands, and his substance is increased in the land. 11 But stretch out your hand now, and touch all that he has, and he will renounce you to your face."

12 God said to Satan, "Behold, all that he has is in your power. Only on himself don't stretch out your hand."

2:

1 Again, on the day when the God's sons came to present themselves before God, Satan came also among them to present himself before God. 2 God said to Satan, "Where have you come from?"

Satan answered God, and said, "From going back and forth in the earth, and from walking up and down in it."

3 God said to Satan, "Have you considered my servant Job? For there is no one like him in the earth, a blameless and an upright man, one who fears God, and turns away from evil. He still maintains his integrity, although you incited me against him, to ruin him without cause."

4 Satan answered God, and said, "Skin for skin. Yes, all that a man has he will give for his life. 5 But stretch out your hand now, and touch his bone and his flesh, and he will renounce you to your face."

6 God said to Satan, "Behold, he is in your hand. Only spare his life."

7 So Satan went out from the presence of God, and struck Job with painful sores from the sole of his foot to his head. 8 He took for himself a potsherd to scrape himself with, and he sat among the ashes. 9 Then his wife said to him, "Do you still maintain your integrity? Renounce God, and die."

1 CHRONICLES 21:

1 Satan stood up against Israel, and moved David to take a census of Israel. 2 David said to Joab and to the princes of the people, "Go, count Israel from Beersheba even to Dan; and bring me word, that I may know how many there are."

3 Joab said, "May God make his people a hundred times as many as they are. But, my lord the king, aren't they all my lord's servants? Why does my lord require this thing? Why will he be a cause of guilt to Israel?"

MARK 1:

12 Immediately the Spirit drove him out into the wilderness. 13 He was there in the wilderness forty days tempted by Satan. He was with the wild animals; and the angels were serving him.

LUKE 10:

17 The seventy returned with joy, saying, "Lord, even the demons are subject to us in your name!"

18 He said to them, "I saw Satan having fallen like lightning from heaven.

JOHN 13:

26 Jesus therefore answered, "It is he to whom I will give this piece of bread when I have dipped it." So when he had dipped the piece of bread, he gave it to Judas, the son of Simon Iscariot. 27 After the piece of bread, then Satan entered into him.

CHAPTER 26

King Saul

■ ■ ■

INTRODUCTION

There is ample evidence in the book of 1 Samuel that Saul was troubled by what we today would call a mental disorder, and what the Bible calls an "evil spirit" (16:14-23). Several writers have tried to diagnose Saul's disturbing state of mind, though none of the published attempts has met with widespread agreement.

The case is not simple, but one clue to the madness may lie in 19:8-17, where the evil spirit comes upon him with especially great force after David's impressive success in defeating the Philistine army with their superior weapons—something Saul at times found difficult. As an apparent result of David's victory, Saul tries to kill David.

Another passage in the same book that adds to this impression is 20:31, where we read of Saul saying to his son Jonathan, "As long as [David] lives on this earth, neither you nor your kingdom will be established. Now send and bring him to me, for he must die."

While the exact nature of Saul's aberrant behavior remains unclear, it is nevertheless obvious enough that he is concerned more for his own success and that of his imagined dynasty than for the survival of Israel or for a strict obedience to the commands of Israel's God.

KING SAUL

MONOLOGUE

They think me mad. I see it in their eyes. Do madmen prophesy? Answer me!

It was at Gilgal. There my luck turned sour. My son set war aflame with Philistines. They came against us like the gross remainder of the world. They camped below our lookouts, their myriad of tents a carpet on the land out to where eye cannot stretch.

My stoutest men were trembling at the sight. Some hid among the rocks, in any hole, in cisterns underground. They picked their way at night for other parts. My army wizened.

I had agreed with Samuel to wait for him, not moving to attack until he'd made an offering. "In seven days," he said, he would return. But seven days were past. I could not lose another day's desertions and keep to me a possibility of waging war. And surely not against an enemy that blew at me like sand, and planned to separate my throat.

Besides, I'd superseded Samuel. He'd said so, and he said "God" told him the same. (He has his dreams, his voices in the night. Don't ask me whose. Perhaps they're from the dead.) Still and all, I had the right I say, and so I called to me the offerings to burn, a kingly sign that would embolden simple men to kill.

Because he had not come in seven days, I burned the offerings as custom said one must. And then I told them to come bleed the meat before we burned and ate it, as is right. Do madmen do such things? I think he lagged to force my innovative sacrifice, resenting my supplanting him. But kings have rights, and I have superseded him.

This boy, whose whole career was tending sheep, this stripling and his lucky stone, was his own, that jackal Samuel's device to push me from my throne. The young camel's nose into my tent was that sweet lyre he strummed to still my nerves, but once inside, his bulging spirit cowed my own. It troubled me. What right had he to tumble down the edifice I'd built, the crowds who'd filled the roads to shout my praise, my officers who watched my face for scowls or hint of smile, and then my promising son. Ah yes, my son.

I could foresee (I am a prophet, am I not?) my kingship as a dynasty, and Jonathan, new seated on my throne, commanding obsequies and buildings to my name. How can a prophet lie? He cannot. Therefore it fell to me to carry out what I'd foretold. This bumpkin David dies!

Therein were told the lies of my crazed skull, my spears and my campaigns against his threat to what was legible in entrails and in stars. You cannot call me mad. I'm not.

KING SAUL

1 SAMUEL 13:

5 The Philistines assembled themselves together to fight with Israel, thirty thousand chariots, and six thousand horsemen, and people as the sand which is on the seashore in multitude. They came up and encamped in Michmash, eastward of Beth Aven. 6 When the men of Israel saw that they were in trouble (for the people were distressed), then the people hid themselves in caves, in thickets, in rocks, in tombs, and in pits. 7 Now some of the Hebrews had gone over the Jordan to the land of Gad and Gilead; but as for Saul, he was yet in Gilgal, and all the people followed him trembling. 8 He stayed seven days, according to the time set by Samuel; but Samuel didn't come to Gilgal, and the people were scattering from him. 9 Saul said, "Bring the burnt offering to me here, and the peace offerings." He offered the burnt offering.

10 It came to pass that as soon as he had finished offering the burnt offering, behold, Samuel came; and Saul went out to meet him, that he might greet him. 11 Samuel said, "What have you done?"

Saul said, "Because I saw that the people were scattered from me, and that you didn't come within the days appointed, and that the Philistines assembled themselves together at Michmash; 12 therefore I said, 'Now the Philistines will come down on me to Gilgal, and I haven't entreated the favor of God.' I forced myself therefore, and offered the burnt offering."

13 Samuel said to Saul, "You have done foolishly. You have not kept the commandment of God, which he commanded you; for now God would have established your kingdom on Israel forever. 14 But now your kingdom will not continue. God has sought for himself a man after his own heart, and God has appointed him to be prince over his people, because you have not kept that which God commanded you."

15 Samuel arose, and went from Gilgal to Gibeah of Benjamin. Saul counted the people who were present with him, about six hundred men.

16:

14 Now God's Spirit departed from Saul, and an evil spirit from God troubled him. 15 Saul's servants said to him, "See now, an evil spirit from God troubles you. 16 Let our lord now command your servants who are in front of you to seek out a man who is a skillful player on the harp. Then when the evil spirit from God is on you, he will play with his hand, and you will be well."

17 Saul said to his servants, "Provide me now a man who can play well, and bring him to me."

18 Then one of the young men answered, and said, "Behold, I have seen a son of Jesse the Bethlehemite who is skillful in playing, a mighty man of valor, a man of war, prudent in speech, and a handsome person; and God is with him."

19 Therefore Saul sent messengers to Jesse, and said, "Send me David your son, who is with the sheep."

20 Jesse took a donkey loaded with bread, and a container of wine, and a young goat, and sent them by David his son to Saul. 21 David came to Saul, and stood before him. He loved him greatly; and he became his armor bearer. 22 Saul sent to Jesse, saying, "Please let David stand before me; for he has found favor in my sight." 23 When the spirit from God was on Saul, David took the harp, and played with his hand; so Saul was refreshed, and was well, and the evil spirit departed from him.

19:

8 There was war again. David went out, and fought with the Philistines, and killed them with a great slaughter; and they fled before him.

9 An evil spirit from God was on Saul, as he sat in his house with his spear in his hand; and David was playing with his hand. 10 Saul sought to pin David to the wall with the spear; but he slipped away out of Saul's presence, and he stuck the spear into the wall. David fled, and escaped that night. 11 Saul sent messengers to David's house, to watch him, and to kill him in the morning. Michal, David's wife, told him, saying, "If you don't save your life tonight, tomorrow you will be killed." 12 So Michal let David down through the window. He went away, fled, and escaped. 13 Michal took the teraphim, and laid it in the bed, and put a pillow of goats' hair at its head, and covered it with clothes. 14 When Saul sent messengers to take David, she said, "He is sick."

15 Saul sent the messengers to see David, saying, "Bring him up to me in the bed, that I may kill him." 16 When the messengers came in, behold, the teraphim was in the bed, with the pillow of goats' hair at its head.

20:

30 Then Saul's anger burned against Jonathan, and he said to him, "You son of a perverse rebellious woman, don't I know that you have chosen the son of Jesse to your own shame, and to the shame of your mother's nakedness? 31 For as long as the son of Jesse lives on the earth, you will not be established, nor will your kingdom. Therefore now send and bring him to me, for he shall surely die!"

32 Jonathan answered Saul his father, and said to him, "Why should he be put to death? What has he done?"

33 Saul cast his spear at him to strike him. By this Jonathan knew that his father was determined to put David to death.

CHAPTER 27

Simon The Magician

■ ■ ■

INTRODUCTION

Human language surely is a part of God's creation, which He called good. And if it is truly his creation and good, then it was created to convey the truth, not to deceive and mislead others in order to dupe them.

But before Jesus ascended to the Father, He left on earth a treasure to his apostles, the power of miraculous healing. The treasure was not literally money, as Simon Magus seems to have thought. The Christian healing miracles were meant to confer a restorative blessing on others, but Simon hungers for their power in order to bless his money bag. If Jesus taught his followers to work for the freeing of others from sin, Simon seems to work only to free others from their wealth, no matter how modest that wealth may be.

What his sins come down to in the end is a flat contradiction of Jesus' answer to the scribes: Simon's type of person loves himself but not his neighbor; and there is no sign that he even recognizes God's true and living existence, let alone loving Him.

And when he tries to *buy* the apostles' apparent power to bestow the Holy Spirit on others, Simon betrays his stubborn refusal to accept the fact that God is not only alive but also *sovereign*, not at all someone to be bought like a slave.

His is not an aberration peculiar to his own time. This compulsion to evaluate everything in terms of money has long been a human trait.

People of his type exist also in the modern world, both in secular and in Christian circles.

SIMON THE MAGICIAN

MONOLOGUE

I fail to understand the hatred some have spat at those of us who long to wield a power greater than the common run of men. Are none to be admired by gaping mouths? What pleasure in a life when no one does the seemingly impossible: a lamb that turns into a rat, a jar of wheat now sand, a newborn daughter changed to nanny goat. These things give flavor like a pinch of salt.

The poor Samaritans, astonished, gave me silver to enact my tricks. My cunning pleased them mightily, and they presumed of me a might that pleased me too. Was this not a fair exchange we made? To walk the roads and with a scowl make cringe the man who heretofore had led the town, or smile at adolescent girls and see obeisance in their eyes—all this and more was paradise to me until my fortune turned and Philip's tricks outdid mine in their eyes. I thought it cautious to blend in with him and learn what joyed the rabble overmuch. He differed subtly, so it took some days.

I cannot lie. It baffled me.

Then came their finest sort, two fishermen, who told the crowd, "Receive the Holy Spirit." I'd never met a spirit with the smallest part of holiness, and doubted that such powers were. But these Samaritans, these surly oafs, these cheats, these trite believing fools, were then transformed to naive "sheep." I knew their wine and bread were drugged, but with no drug I knew from my own pharmacopeia.

I'd heard of Judas, who'd received a bag of silver and was cursed for taking it. I would reverse his fault and give them coins to merely know the potion's name and source. But nothing I could do, no action done with honeyed words and innocence could gain me entry to their stiff cabal. I thought it best to leave in peace, so made a final gesture of good will, to shame the prigs for coldly ostracizing me. I bade them pray for

me and left them with their hands upraised, as if their God could soar
and would, at their request, drop something pure.

SIMON THE MAGICIAN

ACTS 8:

9 But there was a certain man, Simon by name, who used to practice sor-
cery in the city and amazed the people of Samaria, making himself out
to be some great one, 10 to whom they all listened, from the least to the
greatest, saying, "This man is that great power of God." 11 They listened
to him, because for a long time he had amazed them with his sorceries.
12 But when they believed Philip preaching good news concerning God's
Kingdom and the name of Jesus Christ, they were baptized, both men
and women. 13 Simon himself also believed. Being baptized, he continued
with Philip. Seeing signs and great miracles occurring, he was amazed.

14 Now when the apostles who were at Jerusalem heard that Samaria
had received the word of God, they sent Peter and John to them, 15
who, when they had come down, prayed for them, that they might receive the Holy Spirit; 16 for as yet he had fallen on none of them. They
had only been baptized in the name of Christ Jesus. 17 Then they laid
their hands on them, and they received the Holy Spirit. 18 Now when
Simon saw that the Holy Spirit was given through the laying on of the
apostles' hands, he offered them money, 19 saying, "Give me also this
power, that whomever I lay my hands on may receive the Holy Spirit."
20 But Peter said to him, "May your silver perish with you, because you
thought you could obtain the gift of God with money! 21 You have neither part nor lot in this matter, for your heart isn't right before God. 22
Repent therefore of this, your wickedness, and ask God if perhaps the
thought of your heart may be forgiven you. 23 For I see that you are in
the poison of bitterness and in the bondage of iniquity."

24 Simon answered, "Pray for me to the Lord, that none of the
things which you have spoken happen to me."

CHAPTER 28

Thomas Didymus

■ ■ ■

INTRODUCTION

It has been said that honest atheists do not know Christianity well enough to believe in the divinity of Jesus. While this was said many centuries after the time of Christ's life on earth, it can be applied to his disciple Thomas, the disciple who is often called Doubting Thomas.

It is important, that is, to notice that the man who is famous for doubting was in doubt about the Resurrection only until he was presented with evidence that taught him to believe. The evidence, of course, was the actual wounds in Jesus' hands and side. He then believed in the Resurrection so vehemently that he knelt before the risen Lord and proclaimed his divinity. (Note, however, that his fellow disciples, it is implied in Scripture, still believed Jesus to be only the messiah, a prophet and a king, but still only a man.)

It's not easy to overturn long-held evaluations about people. That is what makes first impressions so important. And this is particularly so when these people are no longer around to defend themselves. But it just might be that John (whose gospel is filled with ironies) includes Thomas in his gospel as the skeptic whose eventual belief is stronger evidence for that belief. If the witness is truly a skeptic, then there is no prior agenda in favor of belief, making the witness more credible to outsiders.

At the very least, it is clear that Thomas saw the wounds in the body of a man he recognized as that of Jesus, and that those wounds were real, for he did not put his hands into them, something he earlier said he must do in order to believe. We today have equally compelling physical evidence before our eyes, the millions of people who try to follow Jesus, the world-wide church. They would not have called themselves Christians if there had been no resurrection.

I give you now one version of Thomas speaking of his experiences. Do you hear in him the words of an honest man?

THOMAS DIDYMUS

MONOLOGUE

I tell you straight, I've seen strong men die, and the weeping and prostrate too, lambs of children baffled by the pain while women wail. You want a fact? Death is a fact. When death arrives, everything else aside, as if a bully of a king had lacked a seat, and every good man gave up his. Those fragrances of springtime, friendships at a meal, one's treasure of a wife, some wealth secure, fresh bread, the morning birds, the psalms: all yeast that leavens little pockets of pleasure in a dusty world; as sure and stable in the face of death as breezes or expected harvests. A house of twigs is life.

Then came our rabbi, one good man who could rescind.... But no, I leap ahead. With these two eyes I saw him heal the lame. Madmen he dispossessed of imps, the blind he sighted, on and on. It was a joy to be with him, to see the miseries fall flat, to see the leash He put on pain itself, just walking by and taking note of illnesses.

Then Lazarus of Bethany fell sick and messengers were come, and so the rabbi said he would not die, or something such. That's why we thought absurd his saying two days later, staring at the heavens, "Let's to Judea." Well you should have seen the twelve go taut. Was this another of his parables? Judea, mind you, where they think God's stones were made to crunch a rabbi till he died. Where most cheerfully they nearly slew the only man who ever set so many things to right.

We tried to hold him back, but nothing worked. He spoke some dark things touching daylight and some others touching sleep. Then

He told us: Lazarus was dead. I saw two things: that death was waiting like a beast in Bethany; and death would eat our rabbi. And with that the old, sad sickness of the world rose like a dead sun in the east for me. I fell back on my toughness and I told them pat, "Let's all go. Let's die with him." I thought but didn't say, let's have no pious lies of Pharisees on resurrection, but dumb as stones themselves go all as one with him into the darkness.

I never was more wrong but once.

Still, death collapsed before his powers once again. And He, as trim as a bridegroom, handed Lazarus to life. A godly knack, I thought, for strewing health the way a sower casts the seed. How does He do it? came into my mind. And then it came to me what He had meant when saying He had come from Adonai. But on.

The Passover approached. The rabbi spoke of death in cold consolement as I heard it. We shaken twelve looked on aghast to hear him say that He would die for some vague good I didn't catch. Now? Now that death had cowered at his voice? And then I saw it was a stall back there in Bethany; the monster only waited, held its breath.

They took him, tried him, sold him, beat him till another man would plead, hung him up like food for kites. The rest of us had gone so many turns morale was low. Our courage in exhaustion, it made a balance to retreat or stay with him and suicide, more Roman than a Jew would care to be. Time seemed almost to stop. Some entombed him.

And then one day I'm told the Magdalene got John and Cephas on the run. They thought the body stolen. The men went home. The woman stayed, recalling things He meant to her, when who should greet her but the gardener. To make it short, the gardener was not the gardener. The Rabbi was alive, she said. I knew the type. To keep from going mad they make up such fulfilling balderdash as "other worlds where no one dies." I wanted nothing more of it, or them. So I remained at home.

They brought me food and said He came to them past locks. Don't ask me how. It's not my specialty, this thinking hard about impossibilities like how the dead can turn around and not be dead. I laughed, but they were resolute. They asked me what would make a proof to wipe away my doubts. I said, "The most immediate cause of this ruinous death, his wounds. If I could take him in my hands like any man, as well as ask my eyes, I'd say all right, have done, the world is bright and sweet.

But now my curiosity was up. Next week I joined them behind the fastened doors. I stood staring when He stepped as neat as thinking up to me, said, "Here, in my hands, put your fingers there in place of the nails. Here, in my side, make your hand the spear. Believe!"

I looked at Cephas and our roles looked switched. Time was I could hardly stand his fawning, calling a mere rabbi the Messiah, Lord. Now I was there. If Cephas was a fool, the more fool I. I saw it truly now: the monster sprang and swallowed; its victim's blade cut deep and wide within so that, through dying, death should die. It was too good to be. And yet it was. This was the One who died, and here he was alive and teaching me good sense.

I thought back on the healings and my short attention span, the way the signs became more obvious, and as He waited for my reply, my legs gave way, my eyes dissolved, my breathing came in gusts, and I admitted He was God, asked his forgiveness.

And now, remembering it all, I lust to live again those subtler signs: the crippled and the blind, the touching of his clothes. Or better yet, to never in my life have eyed him, just be told through others' witnessing.

THOMAS DIDYMUS

JOHN 11:

16 Thomas therefore, who is called Didymus, said to his fellow disciples, "Let's go also, that we may die with him."

14:

5 Thomas said to him, "Lord, we don't know where you are going. How can we know the way?"

20:

24 But Thomas, one of the twelve, called Didymus, wasn't with them when Jesus came. 25 The other disciples therefore said to him, "We have seen the Lord!"

But he said to them, "Unless I see in his hands the print of the nails, put my finger into the print of the nails, and put my hand into his side, I will not believe."

26 After eight days again his disciples were inside and Thomas was with them. Jesus came, the doors being locked, and stood in the middle, and said, "Peace be to you." 27 Then he said to Thomas, "Reach here your finger, and see my hands. Reach here your hand, and put it into my side. Don't be unbelieving, but believing."

28 Thomas answered him, "My Lord and my God!"

29 Jesus said to him, "Because you have seen me, you have believed. Blessed are those who have not seen, and have believed."

21:

1 After these things, Jesus revealed himself again to the disciples at the sea of Tiberias. He revealed himself this way. 2 Simon Peter, Thomas called Didymus, Nathanael of Cana in Galilee, and the sons of Zebedee, and two others of his disciples were together. 3 Simon Peter said to them, "I'm going fishing."

They told him, "We are also coming with you." They immediately went out, and entered into the boat. That night, they caught nothing. 4 But when day had already come, Jesus stood on the beach, yet the disciples didn't know that it was Jesus. 5 Jesus therefore said to them, "Children, have you anything to eat?"

They answered him, "No."

6 He said to them, "Cast the net on the right side of the boat, and you will find some."

They cast it therefore, and now they weren't able to draw it in for the multitude of fish.

ACTS 1:

13 When they had come in, they went up into the upper room where they were staying; that is Peter, John, James, Andrew, Philip, Thomas, Bartholomew, Matthew, James the son of Alphaeus, Simon the Zealot, and Judas the son of James. 14 All these with one accord continued steadfastly in prayer and supplication, along with the women, and Mary the mother of Jesus, and with his brothers.

WOMAN CAUGHT IN ADULTERY

CHAPTER 29

The Woman Caught in Adultery

■ ■ ■

INTRODUCTION

This is an unusual passage in many ways. At first glance it seems to be a simple matter of the scribes and Pharisees having taken charge of a woman caught in the act of adultery and brought before Jesus in yet another attempt to trap him. If He merely releases her, He is violating the Law of Moses, which said that adultery must be punished by stoning (Deuteronomy 22:21-22). But if He orders her stoned to death, He could be accused of violating a Roman law which said Rome alone had the power of capital punishment.

When looked into more closely, however, the case looks more complicated. In particular, why is her lover not present to be judged along with her as Deuteronomy 22:22 prescribes? If she is to be stoned for adultery, so is he. Some scholars explain this with the theory that, not only has the husband conspired to have witnesses to catch his wife, but he might have also arranged for the entire scene to take place. If that was the case, the man who was led by the husband to seduce the wife might well resent being judged as an adulterer for his cooperation and consequently blurt out the conspiracy. This might have ruined the Pharisees' trap for Jesus if it had happened soon enough.

It is also interesting (especially if Jesus senses their ploy, as He usually does) that, instead of telling the woman her sins are forgiven, He tells her that He too refuses to accuse her, as the Pharisees have done implicitly by silently leaving the scene.

One more item needs clarifying. When Jesus refuses to accuse the woman, He immediately adds, "Sin no more." This final comment clarifies his dismissal of her. Her agreeing to an act of adultery, even if within a conspiracy unknown to her at the time, was still a sin. He sets aside the sin this time, but she is to commit it no more. If there was a conspiracy, that was his main concern. Do you believe there was a conspiracy?

THE WOMAN CAUGHT IN ADULTERY

MONOLOGUE

When my accusers shoved me at the rabbi, my husband was not there to hear him say that He would not accuse me. Or maybe the rabbi's forgiveness meant nothing to him. Either way, he slapped me hard when I got home.

Then I recalled, when I'd stopped crying, that Jacob also was not there to have his sin with me judged. It was only then I put that together with his being my husband's friend and saw that I'd been lured into a trap.

My youth and my obedience, I think, had made my husband believe I was a fool. And that, I must admit (if I am to be an honest woman now), warmed in me an appetite for revenge. But soon I cooled and saw the rabbi's way was best, to hold in hand forgiveness for the moment he repents (which he never did, or never told me that he did).

I go now to the well to fetch the water there, but not a smile or even a nod from women. The hiss of whispered "hussy" reaches me, and I begin to think these holy matrons all have lived their lives devoid of sin.

But I will never trust another man, and especially not one who brings me pomegranates and sweet dates. And though I'm ready to forgive the trap my husband set for a few silver coins, I will distrust him too.

THE WOMAN CAUGHT IN ADULTERY

JOHN 8:

3 The scribes and the Pharisees brought a woman taken in adultery. Having set her in the middle, 4 they told him, "Teacher, we found this woman in adultery, in the very act. 5 Now in our law, Moses commanded us to stone such women. What then do you say about her?" 6 They said this testing him, that they might have something to accuse him of.

But Jesus stooped down and wrote on the ground with his finger. 7 But when they continued asking him, he looked up and said to them, "He who is without sin among you, let him throw the first stone at her." 8 Again he stooped down and wrote on the ground with his finger.

9 They, when they heard it, being convicted by their conscience, went out one by one, beginning from the oldest, even to the last. Jesus was left alone with the woman where she was, in the middle. 10 Jesus, standing up, saw her and said, "Woman, where are your accusers? Did no one condemn you?"

11 She said, "No one, Lord."

Jesus said, "Neither do I condemn you. Go your way. From now on, sin no more."

Questions for Meditation or Discussion

1. **Abraham** Should Christians admire people like Abraham who make a mistake arising from their impatience to obey God?
2. **Adam** If God knew everything that would happen to us before He made the universe, did He expect the Fall? Did He also approve of it?
3. **Bathsheba** Did Bathsheba manipulate David into adultery for purposes of her own ambition?
4. **Cain** Did God test Cain's heart for his greatest weakness to sin, his anger?
5. **David** How can David, an adulterer and a murderer, be "a man after [God's] own heart"?
6. **Herod Antipas** Why does Herod Antipas seem so poised and self-confident on first reading, while a closer reading reveals a troubled personality? What makes the difference?
7. **Isaac** Isaac's father, Abraham, is extremely faithful to God in, among other things, planning to sacrifice his only son. To whom is Isaac equally faithful while a boy?
8. **Jacob** Jacob wrestled with God, and yet Jacob seems at one point (Gen 32:25) to almost have won the match. How can this be?
9. **Job** 1. Who is in the wrong, Job or God? 2. Elihu says Job has brought his misery upon himself. Is he correct? 3. When God

speaks to Job, is He speaking as a boss who abuses his authority or as a loving father correcting his child?

10. **Jonah** Jonah seems more interested in the punishing of sinners than in persuading them to stop sinning. Has the reader ever felt this desire for extreme sinners?

11. **Joseph and his brothers** What is it about Joseph (in addition to his faith in God) that enables him to forgive his brothers?

12. **Judas** What have you decided was Judas's primary motive in betraying Jesus? Alternatively, was there no *primary* reason, only a "pack" of reasons? What would your reason(s) have been?

13. **Lazarus** How would you have reacted to having been raised from your grave as Lazarus was? Do you think he was grateful or resentful?

14. **Mary of Bethany** In your considered opinion, is it holier to work with one's hands than it is to work at learning about God?

15. **Moses** How is Moses' anger in Exodus 32 more to be applauded than Cain's anger at having his sacrifice rejected by the Lord?

16. **Nathan on David** How do you suppose Nathan came up with the idea of a parable for tapping into David's conscience?

17. **Nicodemus** How does Nicodemus progress from contradicting Jesus to being one of Jesus' disciples?

18. **Noah** If the great Flood was God's way of removing evil from the world, how did evil survive the cleansing process?

19. **Paul** Why do you think Jesus chose a Christian-hater like Saul to transform into a super-Christian like Paul?

20. **Rahab** In a word, how would you describe the prostitute Rahab's overall reputation as the Bible presents her?

21. **Rich Young Ruler** This young man evidently worships (holds in higher esteem than anything else) his wealth. Still, he expects Jesus to applaud him despite his idolatry. Do we keep similar idolatries hidden?

22. **Ruth** What is your reaction to Bible scholarship's interpreting the threshing-floor scene as copulation?

23. **Samson** Was Samson's loss of strength caused by breaking the Nazarite vow (to leave his hair uncut), or was it caused by the cutting itself?

24. **Satan** Was "the satan" essentially different from the later "Satan," or were they alike? If different, how different?

25. **Saul** Is Saul's mental disorder only ambition for founding a dynasty, or is there another component of his irrational behavior?

26. **Simon the Magician** Is Simon, in his eagerness to gain wealth by deceit, a type of modern person?

27. **Thomas** Is "Doubting" Thomas justly named?

28. **Woman Caught in Adultery** Is it reasonable to believe that this woman was the victim of a conspiracy to trap Jesus?

Made in the USA
Middletown, DE
27 July 2015